I0049313

RESCUING THE DOCTOR-PATIENT RELATIONSHIP

RESCUING THE DOCTOR-PATIENT RELATIONSHIP

How To Restore Patient-Centric
Decision-Making Amid Economic
And Regulatory Chaos

Ronald W. Hamner, M. D., FACP

Copyright © 2020 by Ronald W. Hamner, M.D.

Rescuing the Doctor-Patient Relationship

All rights reserved. No part of this publication may be reproduced, distributed or transmitted in any form or by any means, including photocopying, recording, or other electronic or mechanical methods, without the prior written permission of the publisher, except in the case of brief quotations embodied in critical reviews and certain other noncommercial uses permitted by copyright law.

Although the author and publisher have made every effort to ensure that the information in this book was correct at press time, the author and publisher do not assume and hereby disclaim any liability to any party for any loss, damage, or disruption caused by errors or omissions, whether such errors or omissions result from negligence, accident, or any other cause.

Adherence to all applicable laws and regulations, including international, federal, state and local governing professional licensing, business practices, advertising, and all other aspects of doing business in the US, Canada or any other jurisdiction is the sole responsibility of the reader and consumer.

Neither the author nor the publisher assumes any responsibility or liability whatsoever on behalf of the consumer or reader of this material. Any perceived slight of any individual or organization is purely unintentional.

The resources in this book are provided for informational purposes only and should not be used to replace the specialized training and professional judgment of a health care or mental health care professional.

Neither the author nor the publisher can be held responsible for the use of the information provided within this book. Please always consult a trained professional before making any decision regarding treatment of yourself or others.

ISBN 978-1-954066-02-1

Acknowledgements

Thanks go to Mats Wahlstrom for planting the idea of writing a book about influences on decision-making for a patient's medical care. He suggested it while we were sitting in his home in Denver discussing decisions about medical care for his mother, who was hospitalized in Sweden. Thanks to my wife, Rebecca B. Hamner, D.M.D., and daughters, Ellen Fremion, M.D., Melissa Mageroy, Ph.D., and Ashley Thalken, M.B.A., for providing many suggestions and insights for writing, especially the first two chapters. Retired English assistant professor, Mary Berman, M.A., kindly edited the manuscript providing valuable help for the writing. Thanks also to Leanne Moore for copy editing and Lucy Holtsnider for cover design and typesetting.

Contents

ONE

Introduction

The doctor-patient relationship serves as a focusing lens in providing high-quality care for an individual. Understanding the doctor-patient relationship for renal patients, that is, patients with kidney disease receiving expensive, highly regulated care, helps to focus insights applicable to the American health care system. Nephrology, which is the internal medicine specialty treating renal patients, has developed over the past 60 years to a mature medical specialty providing a model for how a health care industry sector develops. Elucidating the development of medical care provision, evolution in payment for medical care, reasons behind the current health care situation, and aspects of the health system vulnerability to failure reveals potentially useful systematic changes for improving the viability of the health care industry. More importantly, disrupting current struggling systems for health care provision and payment stimulates opportunities to improve individualized quality of care while potentially rescuing the American health care system from future bankruptcy.

During the twentieth century, medical care in America transformed from descriptive to prescriptive. That is, early twentieth-century physicians provided acute, comfort-based care rather than chronic care for most diseases, reflecting few curative options. That state of the art is revealed by the era's medical science articles mostly consisting of patient-event journals detailing acute recovery or death. Comfort care inherently resided within the doctor-patient relationship as the physician encouraged or consoled the patient. By the middle of the twentieth century, new pharmaceuticals, and new surgical techniques innovated care, changing short-duration maladies to longer-duration disease states. Prescriptive care ascended in dominance as improvements in curative care options accelerated.

Innovations followed governmental and business money infusion into the American medical system. The torrent of infused money stimulated business development including the hospital industry, pharmaceutical industry, health insurance industry, durable medical goods industry, and others. However, applying innovation to medical care created an increasing financial stress on the patient and payers. Prices for services rose as innovative, prescriptive services used more resources. As innovation in American medical care accelerated, payment systems strained to cover rising prices for delivering advanced care to the patient.

Third-party payers, mostly as health insurance companies and benefit processing companies, poured into the health care system necessitating government regulation for these nonmedical participants in medical care. Indeed, as uncovered costs prompted change from being a regulator, the federal government entered the non-provider area of health care as both a payer and a regulator. Payers and regulators for the payers increasingly impinged on the doctor-patient relationship by steering medical decisions to business matrices and government regulations. Not only were costs adversely affected by the influx of payers and regulators,[1] but payees found an opportunity to beneficially influence payments. Payment recipients, such as hospitals, nursing homes, and pharmacies, capitalized on the opportunity to influence governmental and payer regulations and policies that enhanced revenues. In what was added to business costs and therefore prices, non-provider health care entities spent over 6 billion dollars during the last 20 years lobbying legislators and government regulators for favorable payment systems.[2] The evolving American health care system, affected by innovations, increased costs from innovations and regulation generated outside the point of medical service and impinged on the relationship between the doctor and the patient.

Combining both historical and futurist perspectives about the American health care system should form a social-historical continuum that could inform policy and regulation decisions affecting the business and management of medical care. Examining a medical sector, such as kidney disease care, disproportionately impacted by business costs and government regulation, provides insights applicable to the entire medical industry. Kidney disease patient care illustrates descriptive to prescriptive medical care development over the past century. Furthermore, end stage renal disease (ESRD) patients consume a disproportionately high amount of Medicare dollars while the care has been subjected to 45 years of comprehensive, changing government regulation. Physician interactions with the ESRD patient are many but changed from centering on care provision by the primary care physician to care provided by the nephrologist. However, quality of provided health care for the ESRD patient remains a function of the doctor-patient relationship. Perspective developed during 37 years of nephrology private practice provides insights regarding effects of innovation, regulations generated by nonmedical committees, and intrusions into the doctor-patient relationship on the care of nephrology patients. These insights apply to the broader continuum of medical care in the United States.

Personalized treatment at an affordable price is the concern of every patient. Caring personally for a patient motivates many physicians to enter medical school. Providing excellent treatments utilizing successful innovations reflects a goal of practicing physicians. Under the aegis of the doctor-patient relationship, these aspirations can be focused into a cohesive delivery of desired medical care. However, questions arise when moving medical decisions to a faceless bureaucracy from being made jointly with the physician expert in the patient's major problem and the patient. How can medical care be improved while preserving individualized care? Can providers of medical care be encouraged to innovate during the process of medical care while being cost efficient regarding the use of resources? How can patients be motivated to participate in their own medical care? If the doctor-patient relationship is the best lens to focus efforts providing high-quality care, how can the doctor-patient relationship be rescued and energized to continue provision of "best" medical care? Addressing these questions necessitates understanding the development of the American medical system and nonmedical forces affecting both that system and the doctor-patient relationship. Addressing these questions is part of the search for solutions saving the American medical industry from implosion under the increasing weight of potentially unpayable costs, restrictive regulations, and conversion of the patient from beneficiary of optimized medical care to becoming a commodity in the system.

Care for nephrology patients provides a model and laboratory for addressing the looming crisis for medical care in America. Nephrology patients have incredibly complex medical problems and use a disproportionate amount of medical resources as compared to patients with other diseases. Duration of care for these kidney patients has rapidly changed from a short term of weeks or months to increasingly longer time periods of years. Physician work for chronic kidney disease management now greatly exceeds physician work for acute kidney disease management reflecting prolonged patient survival from months to years to decades as 60 years of innovation transformed renal replacement therapy. Moreover, the expense and technology used in this innovative care led to government impingement on the decisions made by the doctor and patient through payment rules and other regulations. Government payments and regulations providing dialysis care for patients began about 45 years ago. As the ESRD patient population increased, nephrology care costs and regulations have greatly increased. Thus, payer and regulator impact on the provision of medical care and the doctor-patient relationship for the nephrology sector of health care can help analyze how third parties affect provision of medical care. The lessons learned in the realm of nephrology can apply to the whole American health care system.

— TWO —

The Doctor-Patient Relationship

If rescuing the doctor-patient relationship serves as a mechanism enhancing medical care in America, understanding that term precedes formulating steps returning to patient-centric care. However, a simple definition of the complex relationship between a physician and person receiving care remains elusive. More useful to understanding the role of the doctor-patient relationship in American medical care begins with using the legal definition modified and nuanced by multiple contexts and influences.

The doctor-patient relationship has traditionally been the basic focusing mechanism for provision of medical care in the United States. This relationship has a legal definition presented on *Uslegal. com*. The physician-patient relationship can be defined as follows: "A consensual relationship in which the patient knowingly seeks the physician's assistance and in which the physician knowingly accepts the person as a patient."[3]

While the terms "doctor" and "physician" have been expansively construed to be any "health care provider," the combined legal, social, and ethical relationship continues to be a mutually consented contract between a licensed doctor and a patient. The *USLegal.com* definition does not consider nuances in the relationship between the physician and patient including how the relationship is initiated, responsibilities within the relationship, and how medical decisions are made regarding the health care of the patient. The term "knowingly" makes assumptions about the patient and physician that may not uniformly apply at the time health care is engaged. This definition also does not consider the importance of the doctor-patient relationship on health care in general. Indeed, according to psychologist Peggy Rothbaum, "The doctor-patient relationship is a key part, quite possibly the most important part, of health care."[4]

Initiation of the doctor-patient relationship is more a social, interpersonal action than a legal, contract-based action, although a legal relationship is established. Responsibilities within the relationship usually are thought to be only held by the doctor. However, as occurs with any contract, responsibilities are also held by the patient. Different from usual legal contracts, the actions of the patient are variable rather than enumerated. Responsibilities of the patient may vary with the interest, energy, and physical status of the patient. Medical decision power will shift during any doctor-patient relationship between the provider and the patient based on the patient's interest and ability within the context of current societal, cultural, economic, and health insurance factors. For example, in some communities, the patient is the passive recipient of medical care while in other communities, the patient is an Internet-driven selector of medical care. An example regarding the influence of health insurance on medical decision power is the use of a gatekeeping primary care physician to control health care decisions with some insurance plans while other plans allow the patient to choose any participating physician. Despite these variations in responsibilities, the provision of medical care and the quality of provided care remains defined by the interactions between provider and patient within the doctor-patient relationship occurring at the time of medical service. As Dr. Rothbaum reports, "The key to quality care is the doctor-patient relationship."[5] This truth has been lost in the vast data bank of quality reports, health trend reports, value-based payment determinations, and application of regular business practices to the health care business.

Moreover, doctor-patient relationship complexities are nuanced by legal, economic, professional, and personal components. These components are affected by training, experiences, legal requirements, moral-ethical positions, and the degree of engagement by participants within the health care process. The ways that these factors influence the relationship also change depending on the varying status of the patient and the status of the provider.

Legal Components

The legal components of the doctor-patient relationship include requirements imposed by government entities and relational obligations governed by contract law. However, these requirements and obligations indirectly affect that relationship as compared to specified actions found in the business world. Moreover, legal requirements regarding the doctor-patient relationship are sometimes imposed by government and corporate entities, such as insurance companies and health care systems, without regard for internal aspects and agreements within the doctor-patient relationship. Thus, the legal relationship between a doctor and a patient is not simply a freely negotiated contract as compared to a personal services contract.

Such legalities acting as an outside influence on the doctor-patient relationship are exemplified by the requirement to obtain a specific signed permission before performing a blood test for the human immunodeficiency virus (HIV) in Nebraska and New York, as contrasted with all other blood testing allowed by a general or implied consent given by the patient being tested.[6] Those two states require a specific informed consent form for HIV testing signed by the patient. All other states comply with Center for Disease Control and Prevention recommendations that a patient be given the specific opportunity to decline testing without signing a separate consent form as explained on the *CDC.gov* website: "General informed consent for medical care that notifies the patient that an HIV test will be performed unless the patient declines (opt-out screening) should be considered sufficient to encompass informed consent for HIV testing."[7]

In contrast, venipuncture for blood tests is consented to by signing an assignment of billing to insurance or signing an agreement to accept personal billing if insurance declines to pay for the laboratory service. Specified consent for a specific blood test is not part of the usual signed document as the more informal, verbal agreement between the physician and patient is that laboratory tests will be part of the provision or ordering of usual medical care. Declination of specific blood tests by the patient is usually based on cost to the patient rather than the nature of the test. Legal requirements are oriented towards payment mechanisms, usually to a third-party laboratory service, except in this example of the HIV test, which is legally viewed as a civil rights issue or protected personal information issue in Nebraska and New York. The legal requirements in the example of HIV testing supersede informal and formal agreements between the physician and the patient.

Moreover, contract law generally is concerned with establishing legal relationships with specified obligations.[8] Usual written contracts legally establish responsibilities and relationships between two or more people and/or entities that direct subsequent actions. Legal relationships are usually illustrated as written contracts between the participating parties except in the realm of medical care provision within the doctor-patient relationship. Actions, rather than written contracts, frequently establish the legal relationship between a physician and a patient, which is concurrently or subsequently affirmed by signing related legal documents. These health-care-related legal documents include consents for therapy, assignment of medical insurance benefits for billing, directions for handling medical records, and permissions for professional medical discussions with persons other than the patient, assuming the patient is not a minor or a legally deemed incapable person. Action can create a legal relationship for a physician when the physician formulates and/or implements a care plan reflecting a medical decision made about the patient. This legal relationship is established as a contract when a physician undertakes professional work leading to a medical opinion about or a medical action done to the patient.[9]

For example, a fifty-six-year-old woman was brought to the emergency room after being found unconscious in her boarding home room. She was unresponsive and had kidney failure, respiratory failure, hypothermia, and the accumulation of extremely high amounts of acids in the blood. Initially, the patient had no known family contacts and was unable to personally handle consents. After intubation, she was moved to the intensive care unit where dialysis was determined to be necessary. Emergency dialysis treatment was initiated, and subsequent care was continued by the nephrologist (the author) without a formal consent by the patient. Thus, a legal relationship was initiated by the nephrologist between the doctor and patient without voluntary action by the patient. Continued nephrological medical care was the responsibility of the nephrologist during the patient's unresponsive state. One week later, the patient's recovery allowed her consent to maintain the doctor-patient relationship. In this example, a physician action initiated a legal doctor-patient relationship despite the patient's passive status.

Most of the time, voluntary engagement by a patient, in what often is non-specified but legally obligated medical care (e.g. medical care without enumerated actions), is seen when patients take an action allowing examination and rendering of care. A patient's unwritten contract and consent for a doctor-patient relationship is established by participation in receiving medical care. Although a contract between two parties obligates responsibilities to each party, the incurred legal responsibility for the patient is often unstated or ignored.[10] Commonly, an example of engagement by the patient for unspecified actions of medical care leading to a legal relationship is exemplified during an initial nephrology office visit in which the patient states, "I was told that my kidney tests aren't normal and I should see you." While rendering an opinion and care by the physician is expected by the patient in this example, the components of such care are not necessarily specified at the time the patient voluntarily assents to establishing the doctor-patient relationship.

Yet, actions do not always establish a doctor-patient relationship as a contract for medical services. One legal exception to the establishment of legal relationship occurs at an accident scene if the physician renders emergency care without agreeing to continue subsequent care. Such care is protected from being a legal doctor-patient relationship, and a contract by state laws known as Good Samaritan Acts is illustrated by the Hawaii Good Samaritan Act: "Any person who in good faith renders emergency care, without remuneration or expectation of remuneration, at the scene of an accident or emergency to the victim of the accident or emergency shall not be liable for any civil damages resulting from the person's acts or omission, except for such damages as may result from the person's gross negligence or wanton acts or omissions."[11]

Another exception to the establishment of a long-term legal relationship is the informal offering and receiving medical advice during a nonprofessional situation such as a social event or a passing conversation. In these two situations, neither the physician nor the patient acts with the intention to establish a long-term relationship. The importance of service location for establishing the doctor-patient relationship is suggested by these two examples. Also illustrated in these examples is the importance of intention to establish a doctor-patient relationship.

However, acting on an intent to establish a long-term relationship constitutes a legally binding contract between a physician and a patient that may be, initially, unwritten. Signatures by the contracted parties are used to establish billing for services rendered and permissions identifying information recipients rather than to establish a contractual relationship. As the doctor-patient relationship contract may be implied by action rather than a written document, the usual medical care contract is different from the usual business legal contract.

Economic Factors

Economic factors affecting medical decisions and medical care are more complex than the exchange of money during a cashier sale. Payment responsibility of patients influence how medical care is sought. Cash flow into the doctor-owned business affects decisions about which patient groups will be seen. Third-party payers frequently establish prices for rendering care. The payment system itself influences decisions about medical services and processes of care. Each of these factors affects the doctor-patient relationship.

Rising patient-borne costs for medical care impact medical decisions and provision of medical services. Economic influence on the doctor-patient relationship can be seen in patient decisions to obtain or reject treatment and medications as determined by costs when payment is made by the patient. Lack of cash may inhibit someone seeking medical care in a doctor's office. Patients sometimes replace regular doctor visits with visits to urgent care centers or emergency rooms to avoid payments to a physician's office. Apparently bills generated at urgent care centers and emergency rooms are viewed by the patient as less personal responsibility than bills generated at a physician's office. An important factor for the patient decision about using urgent care centers and emergency rooms in lieu of the doctor's office is the duration of the doctor-patient relationship.[12]

Economic factors may also affect the decisions by providers for medical care as seen by physician willingness to treat unfunded patients or underinsured patients. Unfunded patients may be unable to pay the full cost for care while underinsured patients have health insurance paying less than physician costs. Both situations affect the doctor-patient relationship, but the payer regulations can institutionalize underpayment effects on physician business. Medicaid, for example, forbids billing patients 1) the difference between Medicaid payment and billed amount, 2) co-payment stated by a private insurance card, 3) denied claims due to provider failure to follow policy, and 4) any amount if Medicaid is the payer of last resort.[13] Medicaid rules have led some practices to decline seeing patients using Medicaid for medical care payment compared to accepting Medicare and private insurance in 2014.[14] Some medical practices decline seeing unfunded or private payment patients to avoid accumulating potentially uncollectible account balances for such patients. Other medical practices or individual physicians see unfunded patients for a reduced fee but risk recoupment of Medicare payments if the reduced fee is deemed by the Center for Medicare and Medicaid Services (CMMS) to be the usual and customary fee.[15] A few practices restrict service to those who prepay a set price. However, prepaid examples reflect a minority of payment systems and decisions for the physician.

For most patient service payments, physician fees are determined by interactions between the group medical practice or solo practitioner and third-party payers instead of negotiations between the doctor and the patient. Such third-party payment systems make the economic aspects of the doctor-patient relationship different from usual commerce and buyer-seller interactions. Unlike most fee-for-service transactions in the commercial world, the price for doctor services usually is not published, especially after the advent of health insurance with assignment of benefits. Negotiations about prices usually occur between third-party payers and the medical practice as a corporate entity rather than between the patient and the doctor. These prices are defined by service codes for the intensity or nature of rendered care. Therefore, when billing for the patient visit, many physicians, rather than basing the bill on rendered medical care, think of service level codes as defined by the federal government via Medicare[16] rather than prices. Medicare establishes the price for each service code by regulation after receiving recommendations from selected sources and government-mandated process hearings.[17] The effect of Medicare policy on physician prices for medical services expands beyond the Medicare beneficiary population.

To set prices when Medicare does not participate as the primary payer, physicians and non-Medicare third-party payers tend to utilize Medicare billing definitions and fee schedules to establish "fair market value" for medical services. The rules determining "fair market value" are imprecise as seen in a discussion by Kirk Rebane during a 2011 educational conference for the Radiology Business Management Association:

> For a service agreement, 'general market value' is defined as 'the compensation that would be included in a service agreement as the result of bona fide bargaining between well-informed parties to the agreement who are not otherwise in a position to generate business for the other party' at the time of the service agreement.
>
> The fair market price is the compensation that has been included in bona fide service agreements with comparable terms at the time of the agreement, where the price or compensation has not been determined in any manner that takes into account the volume or value of anticipated or actual referrals.
>
> Fair market value is defined by the American Society of Appraisers in their Business Valuation Standards, which

closely parallels the definition set forth by the IRS in their
Revenue Ruling 59-60, as the price, expressed in terms of cash
equivalents, at which property would change hands between
a hypothetical willing and able buyer and a hypothetical
willing and able seller, acting at arm's length in an open and
unrestricted market, when neither is acting under compulsion
to buy or sell and when both have reasonable knowledge of
the relevant facts.[18]

Mr. Rebane's presentation in 2011 emphasized basing fees on
market surveys and pricing schedules that reduce the risk for
incurring attention from government and insurance auditors. Prices
and payments above these surveyed prices can be deemed, as seen
in the case of *American Lithotripsy Society v. Thompson*, 2002, to
be fees for inducing referrals[19] rather than fair-market pricing for
services rendered. Notice that patients are not mentioned in these
price-setting processes. Patients often learn of the final price for
services after the insurance plans have disallowed billing amounts,
paid a contracted amount, and/or referred any further payments to
the patient. Medicare may send an informational statement to the
patient listing services paid without explaining the billing codes and
titles justifying the payments. These statements can be confusing as
they usually summate all medical charges and payments including
those to hospitals, physicians, home care agencies, medical equipment
companies, and other entities. Because billing and payment cycles
over a month or more, the patient may learn of the medical care
prices charged, amounts paid, and residual balance owed weeks to
months after the medical service is rendered.

Also, often outside patient control, the third-party payment
mechanism covering physician charges can be an economic influence
tying remuneration to physician behavior by mandating algorithm
use when ordering medications, tests, and other services. Buff and
Terrell suggest that third-party payment mechanisms increase

costs by removing free-market economic interactions between the physician and the patient[20]. The Buff article avers that payments made solely by the patient for cosmetic or laser-based eye treatments improved services for a lower price because the fee was negotiated by the patient and the physician. That is, both cost and quality of medical care benefited when the medical choice was made within the doctor-patient relationship.

Such fee-for-service payments remitted by the patient directly to the physician, however, are not the only or most common mechanism by which physicians in America are paid. Payment mechanisms for most physicians usually fall into three broad categories. Each payment mechanism can have differing effects on physician behavior. Payments can be 1) a prepaid system as in capitation or concierge plans, 2) salaried plans which incentive utilizing employee physicians, or 3) traditional practice plans accepting fee-for-service payments. These fee-for-service payments are usually paid by a third party, such as a health insurance company, but may be paid as cash and cash equivalents by the patient.

Capitation plans involve predetermined monthly or annual payments which are, as required by the Health Maintenance Act of 1973, subject to some type of provider risk for financial loss. The risk is usually assessed as a percentage withhold of principal payment or a recoupment process affecting the physician's total remuneration tied to physician performance. Physician underperformance compared to payer-stipulated goals results in the physician losing the withheld money or facing a repayment to the plan.[21] Some capitation plans may have bonus payment provisions for meeting the goals set by the payer. The American College of Physicians (ACP) gives a definition for capitation in an article by Alguire:

> Capitation is a fixed amount of money per patient per unit of time paid in advance to the physician for the delivery of health care services. The actual amount of money paid is determined

by the ranges of services that are provided, the number of patients involved, and the period of time during which the services are provided. Capitation rates are developed using local costs and average utilization of services and therefore can vary from one region of the country to another. In many plans, a risk pool is established as a percentage of the capitation payment. Money in this risk pool is withheld from the physician until the end of the fiscal year. If the health plan does well financially, the money is paid to the physician; if the health plan does poorly, the money is kept to pay the deficit expenses.[22]

Full-risk capitation means the medical practice receives a larger sum of money to pay all the medical costs for a patient enrolled into that practice over a specified time. These full-risk capitation payments are used to pay for primary care visits, immunizations, medications, hospitalizations, post-hospital care, durable medical equipment, utilization of consulting physicians, and laboratory studies. Solvency of a medical practice tied to full-risk capitation reflects profitability dependent on the medical practice having many patients. The large panel of patients ensures that expenses for patients requiring costly care will be offset by savings for patients whose care costs less than expected. Some capitation payment plans pay a smaller total amount intended to cover only subspecialty physician time and physician office costs. The smaller payment plans can be offered to individual physicians or small group practices without a large group of patients. If the standard for payer-stipulated quality of care is met, money not spent from the lump sum allotment may constitute a bonus for the physician group and physicians. "Risk" is a required component with capitation payment systems that may result in obligation for physicians to cover excess costs or provide additional patient care without remuneration. The amount of risk carried by a physician or physician group is related to the amount of responsibility accepted to manage all or part of patient care for the group of patients covered by the plan.[23]

Like capitation payment plans, concierge plans involve prepayment for medical services although they do not carry additional financial risk for physician responsibility for a patient's total health-care costs. In concierge plans, the physician or practice is prepaid per year for twenty-four-hour availability of a physician as a primary medical care provider for that patient. Covered medical services are usually enumerated at the time of payment. This type of practice can also be called a Direct Pay Medical Practice (DPMP) although DPMG may involve patient payment of fee-for-service per session.[24] The care is usually provided in a medical office but may include house calls. Medical care not provided by the concierge physician is paid by a different mechanism and is not directly linked to the concierge physician remuneration. The concierge payments are usually not covered by health insurance companies. Patients pay the cost for the concierge physician unless the program is covered as a corporate health benefit. Usually, only primary care services are provided, but some concierge practices provide in-office minor surgery, hospital care, some laboratory services, some medications, and contracts with other health-care providers to reduce costs for some services.[25]

In these capitated insurance and concierge payment plans, physicians' services are paid without regard to the time or complexity of the care rendered. In such a payment system, the individual physician within a group practice may receive a salary plus a bonus from the total revenue to the group proportionate to the number of patients empaneled for that physician. Other factors affecting physician bonus payments may include quality-care ratings, committee participation, and patient satisfaction ratings. Bonus payments are made only from the prepaid or allotted monies to the practice for the agreed coverage period, usually one year. Fee-for-service factors do not directly influence the total number of doctor-patient interactions, and, therefore, do not influence total payments for medical care provided by the group of physicians or solo practice concierge physician.

Within capitation and concierge medical care payment plans, doctor-patient interaction varies from a close, personal, ongoing relationship with a concierge physician to a brief, highly time-controlled visit with an employee physician working under a productivity quota. In the capitated insurance model known as a Health Maintenance Organization (HMO), physician incentives for medical decisions may be aligned with common business principles seeking to maintain solvency and profitability of the practice and/or health-care network. Aligning medical decision-making with business principles rather than with the doctor-patient relationship contributed to the failure of HMO health care as controlled by the health insurance industry in the 1990s.[26]

In contrast, concierge medical practices, which usually offer only primary physician services, enable more time to be spent with the patient. Business goals and decisions within the practice tend to have less interference on the attention given by the doctor to the patient. Such unimpaired attention can enhance the doctor-patient relationship. In the concierge practice model, the doctor-patient relationship intensifies concerning usual care and making outpatient medical decisions although this relationship tends to be disrupted by hospitalizations and care provided outside the primary physician's office. The disruption occurs because the concierge physician tends to provide patient care only in the primary care office setting and has less influence on medical decisions made when the patient is treated at another site such as a hospital.

In contrast, physicians employed outside of any private practice and outside of prepaid or concierge plans usually have a payment system combining a salary with incentive payments. Employment may be through teaching institutions (medical schools), government-run health systems (Veterans Administration or Indian Health Service), and hospital systems that purchased physician practices or contracted for in-hospital practices. Doctor-patient relationships within these kinds of physician payment systems vary three general ways. First, a very personal ongoing interaction with a primary care or specialty physician in a chronic disease clinic with a limited number of patients may allow an intense interaction between the physician and the patient. Intense, caring doctor-patient relationships can occur through clinics providing recurrent care for complex or special-need patients requiring shared decision-making to maximize benefit and resource allocation for successful health care. Secondly, brief, time-controlled visits based on business models using an employee physician may be used to produce a high volume of short-duration patient visits increasing fee-for-service billing events. As a result of brief, time-controlled visits, the doctor-patient relationship may become superficial and utilitarian reflecting the limited time spent with each patient.

A different effect on the doctor-patient relationship can be found in teaching hospitals, government-run health care facilities, and hospitalist practices where institution-employed and contracted physicians rotate responsibilities, either weekly or monthly. Rotating patient care responsibility results in different physicians providing treatment during a hospitalization and associated outpatient clinic visits, which disrupts the long-term doctor-patient relationship. As an unintended consequence, the rotating medical care system may produce physicians who easily terminate the doctor-patient relationship learned by pivoting off a patient-care service and, subsequently, never seeing the patient again. Stability and interactions within the doctor-patient relationship can be affected by the physician employment mechanism.

These physician payment methods can also influence physician behavior concerning health-care dollar expenditures. That is, physician choices to order medical tests or therapies may be affected by physician employment. Physicians who participate in business budgeting processes for a health-care system make decisions about money allocations that affect a patient's health care. Such business-based budgeting decisions may align treatment choices more with business solvency and profitability than with maximizing patient treatment alternatives. Other business decisions may be made by the employer (hospital, insurance plan, medical business) that could instruct and/or incentivize the physician to reduce medical service costs by restricting services. As a hospital-employed physician or as a medical-school employed mentor physician, the physician may be disconnected from medical service costs by lack of knowledge about the prices charged.[27] Medical costs may also be disregarded for "sake of teaching" or doing "everything" possible for an assumed malpractice protection benefit.[28] Thus, the physician-employment system may produce physicians who order therapy and medical tests without knowing or considering costs. In general, when the physician is in this kind of employment, the doctor-patient relationship may not be the major factor influencing expenditures reflecting medical decisions.

Yet, economic aspects of traditional private practice affect the doctor-patient relationship differently. Some practices accept only direct payment for a fee-for-service visit, which limits the patients' visits to times when money is available. Most practices accept insurance payments covering the fee for patient care. The fee paid is set by contract with health insurance plans or, concerning Medicare and Medicaid plans, government fiat while frequently requiring some co-payment by the patient. Payments to physicians outside of contracted relationships are usually reduced or not paid resulting in transfer of payment responsibility to the patient unless the physician fee is limited by contract or law. Requirement to make a co-payment, deductible payment, or out-of-network payment by the patient may produce a debtor relationship if the patient incurs an outstanding balance owed to the physician. However, patient care is usually continued by physicians regardless of the monies owed especially when longstanding balances can be "written off" as a bad debt corporate tax deduction.

On the other hand, conflict about maintaining a certain doctor-patient relationship may be generated for the physician when economic pressure mounts for ensuring solvency as a small business owner with ongoing bills coming due. Every patient needs to generate revenue for the business expenses for practicing medicine. Physician office costs usually include employment of seventeen to eighteen people for every 100,000 claims submitted[29] to submit and follow patient bills for services rendered. Other fixed costs include rent, malpractice insurance, and business insurance. Variable costs include supplies, equipment purchases, and, partially, utilities. Professional dues and certification expenses also contribute to business overhead. Charging for office-based services and medications can supplement revenue, but the main mechanism to raise revenue in private practice is increasing the number of patient visits per day, usually on a fee-for-service basis. Depending on solvency of the practice, the doctor-patient relationship can be pressured, as visit time is shortened to increase the number of billable encounters. Time constraints can affect the physician's demeanor during an encounter with a patient. A physician with a harried demeanor from concern about practice costs will have less time and energy to invest into the doctor-patient relationship.

Professional Factors

Professional influence on the doctor-patient relationship is seen in how training and mindset (the intent of the physician to provide good medical outcomes with and within the team of health-care workers providing care for the patient) of the physician affect caring for complex or emotionally taxing patients. Training when I was in medical school at Vanderbilt University from 1974 to 1978 did not consider the question of complexity to be an issue separate from general patient care. General information about diseases was taught in formal sessions with the information clarified and focused through informal, small-group sessions using a patient as the stimulus for learning. Attention to patients with complex medical conditions was taught in the context of an understanding of how complex pathophysiology and subsequent therapy affect the patient. This cognizance was focused by a mentor emphasizing care for the patient, regardless of complexity of the disease. The mentor also taught compassionate interaction with the patient during the duration of the disease state or hospital stay. Mentors included medical school faculty members, doctors in fellowship or residency training, and, occasionally, fellow medical students. Training was basically an apprenticeship-style teaching about how to apply scientific information to medical care with compassion. Physician mindset development during the 1970s and 1980s was frequently internally generated by the doctor-in-training who was intent on avoiding the embarrassment of an incorrect diagnosis or poorly managed patient treatment plan. My definition of professionalism, developed during training, was that it is my responsibility to understand the disease process, the interaction of therapy with the disease, and the patient so that I could best care for any patient irrespective of the disease complexity.

More recently, realization has occurred that professional training to care for complex and emotionally taxing patients is incomplete, reflecting a need for a multidimensional definition of complexity.[30] That is, training a physician to care for the complex patient begins with defining complexity. As Sheri Porter reported in the *American Association of Family Practice News*, "the term 'complex' can be elusive and not easily defined."[31] The difficulty preparing physicians to provide complex care without defining that concept is illustrated by anemic attempts to address such medical training during the past decade. A 2010 comprehensive plan to change the care for medically complex patients by the Australian Medical Association did not address professional training.[32] Training for health care workers addressing complex medical problems was funded with five billion British pounds by the United Kingdom in 2013. However, training was mainly about "foundation level dementia" but not for medical care covering persons with multiple chronic diseases. The remainder of the five billion British pounds was used to increase the number of general health-care workers.[33] A conference about the complex patient seen in the emergency room was given by the Emergency Care Research Institute (ECRI) in 2014. The conference did not cover professional training of physicians how to approach complex medical conditions but included some aspects of professional mindset about patient care.[34] A 2016 article from Ireland concluded that in medical school, this issue of training physicians to care for complex patients remains poorly addressed. The authors proposed a new curriculum content to remedy that deficit.[35] Interestingly, an editorial by Dr. Michael LaCombe in 2018 advocates the apprenticeship model by using a fictional narrative illustrating how medical student teaching and learning by example might occur.[36] Currently, enhanced professional training about complex patients enhancing development of a professional mindset about care for complex patients remains an apprenticeship process dependent on exposure to mentors who think comprehensively and compassionately about the patient.

However, assessing the competence of physicians to care for complex patients has not been ignored by licensing boards. The influence of professional training on a physician's ability to care for a patient is assessed by standardized testing. Privileges for physicians to practice medicine may be granted or withheld based on certifications by official certifying boards. Standardized testing attempting to certify information learned as a qualification for subsequent training and/or jobs has been part of American culture since the idea of testing arose in 1838.[37] Board certification in American medicine began in 1917 as a protection mechanism for established ophthalmology practices from partially trained ophthalmologists entering that work force. Subsequently, such certification became a means to confirm successful academic learning of doctors upon completion of post-graduate training.[38] Preparing to take the certifying exam was an intense process of study that also helped to focus lessons learned during residency and/or fellowship. As a measurement used to standardize physician credentialing, board certification became a factor for inclusion on hospital staffs, on the provider list for some health insurance plans and for eligibility to become a medical director. For nephrologists, certification in nephrology by the American Board of Internal Medicine (ABIM) became a prerequisite for being a Medicare-certified dialysis clinic medical director, which was required to operate a dialysis clinic.[39] However, certifying boards began to question the utility of a single certification test, assessing a physician's fund of knowledge and ability to think on the day of the test, for assuring ongoing competence of that physician. The ABIM certifying board developed the Maintenance of Certification (MOC) process aiming to ensure continuing medical education for the physician by placing a ten-year expiration date on internal medicine and subspecialty certification starting in 1990.[40] The MOC-mandated processes essentially ignored state licensing board continuing education requirements and a person's professional initiative to maintain knowledge and skill. Thus, the ABIM deemed formal professional training, as a beneficial influence on the physician's ability to care for a patient, to be a transient effect, thus necessitating recertification of knowledge through the MOC process.

Nevertheless, MOC validity for certifying professional competence has recently been questioned, which is analogous to the criticisms raised about mandated student testing by the No Child Left Behind Act of 2002 (NCLB). NCLB was criticized for changing curriculum to "teach to the test" rather than teach to educate.[41] Another effect of NCLB was forced removal of veteran teachers who did not have mandated professional teaching credentials.[42] NCLB expired in 2007. However, NCLB effects persisted until passage of Every Student Succeeds Act of 2015 (ESSA), which continued standardized testing but transferred consequence determination for poor test results back to the states[43] as school policy regulators recognized that test results, and consequences attached to those results, reflect local rather than global factors. Similar to the NCLB effect, with the MOC, global and academic care rather than individual patient care has been emphasized in the testing as shown by a 2017 analysis. For general internal medicine doctors taking the recertification exam after ten years of practice, exam questions relevant to conditions seen in usual internal medicine practices comprised only 69 percent of the total questions.[44] This exam emphasis is analogous to a "teaching to the test" effect of NCLB on school curriculum in that the MOC emphasized academic knowledge rather than practical knowledge used in daily patient care.

Another criticism of the medical board certification process revolves around the apparent lack of correlation between MOC process and quality of patient care while testing organizations sought enactment of mandatory reexaminations purchased from those testing organizations. The certifying boards sought to tie recertification of physicians to maintenance of professional practice privileges. In 2014, a study of Veterans Administration physicians showed no correlation for patient outcomes with MOC or lack thereof.[45] Recertification, however, was found to be expensive as the average cost of MOC for the general internist in 2015 was $23,607. For all general internists in the United States, costs were projected to total $5.7 billion over ten years.[46] Ninety percent of the costs accrued from lost productivity and test preparation conferences. A conflict of interest was found by investigative reporter Kurt Eichenwald, who reported that ABIM paid $390,000 between 2009 and 2014 to a Washington, D.C., lobby firm.[47] Congress subsequently passed two laws beneficial to the ABIM reflecting lobbyist desires. Both the Patient Protection and Affordable Care Act (ACA) in 2010 and the Medicare Access and CHIP Reauthorization Act of 2015

(MACRA) incentivized physicians to complete MOC under the ABIM rules. Eichenwald implies that these federal incentives pressure physicians to pay for MOC to secure future payments for Medicare patients. Analogous to the effect of NCLB on the teaching profession, established physicians may leave practice rather than spend the time and money for MOC.

Conversely, such certifications do not guarantee professionalism. Physician professionalism, reflecting a medical professional mindset, has a complex effect on the doctor-patient relationship because such professionalism for a physician is complex. Certifying competency regarding a complex skill starts with defining that skill. Professionalism for physicians has been defined as the following: "Professional competence is the habitual and judicious use of communication, knowledge, technical skills, clinical reasoning, emotions, values, and reflection in daily practice for the benefit of the individual and community being served."[48] However, this definition seems to be sterile, cold, and incomplete.

At McGill University and Ottawa University in Canada, a more complex concept of physician professionalism is taught. As seen in the following diagram by Drs. Richard and Sylvia Cruess, presented at the Ian Hart Conference sponsored by the Canadian Association for Medical Education in 2006, physician professionalism amalgamates professional behaviors with a healer's purposes and activities. Their diagram depicts the interaction between behaviors and activities. These attributes, as formulated by the Drs. Cruess, interact with an implied social contract for medical professionalism between the physician and society to work for the good of that society.[49] The assertion at the University of Ottawa is that the practice of medicine is a "moral endeavor which demands integrity, competence, and high ethical standards among other key attributes."

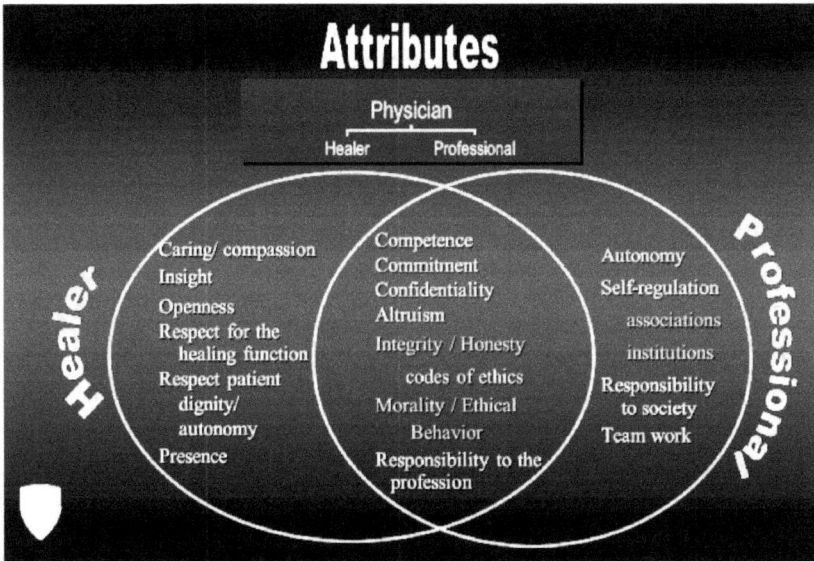

Figure 1. From The Association of Faculties of Medicine of Canada

Regarding medical professionalism, the attributes were reduced to a set of teachable components at the University of Ottawa. However, it has been acknowledged that recognizing the presence of unprofessional behavior in medical school more commonly predicts post-graduation unprofessional behavior compared to any other educational processes or curricula.[50]

The healer's purposes and activities can be interpreted as humaneness. Failure of the medical teaching process to instill humaneness as part of physician professionalism is explored by Atul Gawande in *Being Mortal: Medicine and What Matters in the End*.[51] Doctor Gawande's book presents the argument that medical professionalism is different from knowledge about the body, compliance with national guidelines, or skill in delivering a treatment. Medical professionalism involves connecting with the patient's self-assessment and desires for the future. Being humane is integral to the doctor-patient relationship, reflecting concern for the patient as a person having short- and long-term life goals.

Subsequently, these attempts to define medical profession-alism in terms of curriculum teaching points appear to neglect two personal characteristics that meld the professional and healer components. These two characteristics are fierceness and humility, which are required for appropriate medical professional action within the doctor-patient relationship. Fierceness describes the total commitment to both the therapeutic and best personal interests of the patient. Protectiveness for the patient against payer, provider, and, occasionally, patient's demands counterproductive to the patient's care, patient's optimal comfort, and the patient's expressed goals should provoke physician behavior equivalent to the proverbial she-bear protecting her cubs. Fierceness may also come to play when dealing with unrealistic expectations that lead the patient and family to demand therapy that would likely prolong suffering while offering little benefit. Fierceness incorporates knowledge of what Edmund Pellegrino describes as the patient's "state of unusual vulnerability," which "imposes de facto moral obligations on the physician."[52] The "physician has the obligation to protect the patient's vulnerability against exploitation" based on this "inescapable vulnerability."[53] As patient exploitation can be in the form of adherence to care algorithms or maintaining ineffective treatment programs, fierce physician protection of the patient is a moral obligation of the doctor.

Besides fierceness, humility is also required for the physician professionalism since good intentions do not equal desired outcomes. Humility leads to recognition that some medical problems exceed one physician's capability, and the care must, therefore, be shared with or transferred to another health-care professional. Humility also leads to recognition that well-intended therapeutic actions can lead to injury or death. Treating diseases inherently invokes risk for failure. Indeed, humility acknowledges the reality that every physician who is active in caring for patients has at some time done or not done something that led to an undesired outcome for a patient. Humility is the mindset that appropriates lessons from such costly and emotionally jarring experiences into decision-making by the professional. Without humility, it is difficult to convert experience with patient care into wisdom that is brought to the doctor-patient relationship.

Medical training, continually acquiring knowledge, and developing a medical professional mindset are important for being a health-care provider. However, professionalism in health care requires more that those three aspects of building a medical professional. These components for building a medical professional provide fundamental components for being a doctor. However, more is required to combine these three aspects into what is needed for personalized medical care. Recognizing and embracing the strength (fierceness) and vulnerability (humility) needed for medical professionalism incentivize physicians to maximize the attributes of being professional and a healer in the doctor-patient relationship.

Personal Factors

Personal factors influence both members of the doctor-patient relationship and include biases, emotional stability, and life expectations that may be realistic or unrealistic. The interactions of these influences within the doctor-patient relationship are complex. Also, affecting these interactions is the assumption by all participants in the health-care process that "high-quality medical care" is always provided. Unfortunately, the definition of "high-quality medical care" varies or remains implied rather than defined. As provision of "high-quality medical care" influences how personal factors affect the doctor-patient relationship, the meaning of that term should be explored.

Defining high-quality medical care, especially as such care impacts personal factors within the doctor-patient relationship, is difficult because most quality medical care definitions ignore how the doctor-patient relationship affects the decisions about medical care. Definitions of high-quality medical care usually focus on measurements or global but nonspecific terms as found on the Center for Medicare Advocacy website:

> The U.S. Institute of Medicine (IOM) defines 'quality' as: the degree to which health services for individuals and populations increase the likelihood of desired health outcomes and are consistent with current professional knowledge. What this really means is that each individual consumer should receive the best possible health care available every time services are needed. Health care providers should provide care that meets the needs of each individual patient, including the use of appropriate advances in medical technology. Health care should also be nondiscriminatory, providing the same quality of service regardless of race, ethnicity, age, sex or health status.[54]

Missing in the Center for Medicare Advocacy definition is social context, patient desires, and factors affecting feasibility to undergo evaluation and receive any specific treatment. The Center for Medicare Advocacy definition also uses undefined superlatives of "desired health outcomes" and "best possible health care." On the *Health.gov* website, health-care quality is equated to "keeping patients safe in health care settings,"[55] which neglects information about patient-specific and patient-determined outcomes. More commonly, quality medical care is equated to quality assurance measurements as reported online in the Small Business Chron: "The term 'quality assurance' means maintaining a high quality of health care by constantly measuring the effectiveness of organizations that provide it."[56]

The issue in defining high quality medical care is not a need for measurements. Indeed, assessment of a patient's medical status and the benefits from advancements in medical therapeutics necessarily uses measurements. Thinking about medical care for a patient or a group of patients requires real and verifiable data, that is, measurements. The fallacy occurs when statistical measurements are made the goal for providing high-quality medical care rather than being accepted as tools for assessing patient status and changes in that status.

However, measurements have been used without method validation to determine payment for quality of care. Group statistical measurements rather than individual patient-based outcomes are used to adjust fee-for-service payments mandated by the Medicare and CHIP Reauthorization Act of 2015 (MACRA).[57] Measurements that are basically statistical tools have been turned into quality goals affecting physician payments by this legislation. The fallacy of using measurement tools as goals is demonstrated in the anemia outcomes for dialysis patients as reported by Michael Lazarus and others in 2003.[58] Over the six years reported in that study, anemia results were sorted into quartile groups based on hemoglobins measured for each patient. Each quartile was arbitrarily ranked as being very undesirable, undesirable, desirable, or very desirable. The percentages of all patient hemoglobin measurements in each outcome quartile for anemia remained unchanged year to year. However, individual patient findings frequently showed the patient's standing changed from one quartile to another quartile. These findings show that statistical results for groups do not necessarily show an individual patient outcome. Measurements alone do not define high-quality medical care.

What needs to be added to the definition of high-quality medical care is suggested in an article by Dr. Danielle Ofri. She states:

> I thought about these nurses and doctors when I came across a recent study that found that patient outcomes (in this case, preventing readmission to the hospital after being discharged) were correlated more strongly to the "fuzzy"

measure of patient satisfaction than to the standard "objective" measures of quality.

Patient satisfaction can be an amorphous thing to quantify. But typically, when someone expresses satisfaction with a doctor's care and would recommend him or her to someone else, it usually includes those "soft" attributes like attentiveness, curiosity, compassion, diligence, connection and communication.[59]

Combining the "fuzzy" and "objective" data to benefit medical decision making is best done within the doctor-patient relationship where the soft attributes manifest. Personalizing high-quality medical care means working for the patient to live as well as possible for as long as possible within the context of the patient's health status, prognosis, and health goals. Evidence about disease processes and therapeutic effectiveness must be used to rank diagnostic and treatment options when making medical decisions. Thereby, the patient, with the physician, is allowed opportunity to make an intelligent and compassionate choice about health treatment. Thus, high-quality medical care reflects "fuzzy" desired results measured using objective data focused by the doctor-patient relationship.

Personal interactions have the most complex effect on the doctor-patient relationship. These interactions within the relationship are often determined by the patient, who tends to see the physician as a confidante or confessor. As confidentiality is usually assumed by both parties to be stronger than the confidentiality of the traditional client-lawyer privilege, physicians may be told personal secrets, family secrets, or personal fantasies withheld from other people. Patients expect revealing such normally undisclosed information will not adversely impact the provision of medical care. Physicians share the expectation that knowing the patient's most personal secrets will not adversely impact the objectivity in providing treatment and compassion for the patient. Physicians generally mirror the expectation to be nonjudgmental about the patient after such disclosures are revealed while acting compassionately when subsequently encouraging behavioral changes that promote better health status. Moreover, physician care and physician professionalism are expected to remain untainted despite a patient's unwillingness or inability to change secret or overt self-harming behavior. How personal interactions are handled within the doctor-patient relationship determines the patient comfort in (a) seeing a physician, (b) patient openness to discuss medical problems within the patient's social context, and (c) patient willingness to follow the treatment program.

At the heart of the issue, the patient desires recognition of singularity, that is, being a unique person. A theme throughout the book *Through the Patient's Eyes: Understanding and Promoting Patient-Centered Care,* centering care on the patient occurs when the patient is seen and treated as an individual with a unique set of expectations, understandings, and desires.[60] Such a relationship leads to bonding between the physician and patient so that, sometimes, an expectation develops for physician participation in milestone events for the patient such as birthday celebrations, weddings, and funerals. Many times, confidential personal information revealed within these personal interactions affect medical decision-making and may be crucial for arriving at the best medical decision for a patient's care and protection. The protection of personal confidentiality is not the same issue as legal protection of identifying data and personal information as addressed by the Health Insurance Portability and Accountability Act of 1996. Instead, confidentiality expectation is based on the physician's integrity protecting what is revealed through recorded and unrecorded discussions between the patient and the physician. Complex personal interactions vary and cannot be easily quantified but must recognize the singularity of the patient within the doctor-patient relationship

The doctor-patient relationship provides a patient context helping stratification of treatment options, which determines quality care.

An example of patient context effect on treatment decision is the difference in anticoagulation use for heart problem of atrial fibrillation. For an otherwise healthy fifty-five-year-old man who develops chronic atrial fibrillation but wishes to maintain an active lifestyle, anticoagulation is a treatment option to prevent strokes. With a single disease process, scientific studies and a desire to continue an active lifestyle favor using anticoagulant drugs in the fifty-five-year-old man. In contrast, use of anticoagulant drugs for a seventy-year-old woman with diabetes, kidney failure requiring dialysis, and chronic liver dysfunction invokes a different thought process as activity and life expectancy are different from the fifty-five-year-old man example. While for middle-aged men with atrial fibrillation, stroke prevention therapy has been studied, anticoagulant use in the older, diabetic, cirrhotic, dialysis patients has not been scientifically studied regarding outcomes over five years. In fact, dialysis patients generally carry a high risk for complications when using anticoagulant drugs, which inhibits performing studies about stroke prevention with anticoagulant medications in that group. Both patients incur risk for using an anticoagulant medication, but desired outcome, degree of risk using medication, and potential for avoiding undesirable complications without medication differ. The decision for using an anticoagulant drug or any therapy must be contextualized by the patient's status and therapeutic goals, which is best understood through the doctor-patient relationship.

Understanding how legal, economic, professional, and personal components influence the doctor-patient relationship help fulfill the desire to provide high-quality medical care but do not directly address the cost of that care. Cost of medical care led to payment systems and subsequent regulatory systems as means to deal with expenses. However, the payment and regulation systems affect the American health care system externally to the doctor-patient relationship. How medical care and payment/regulation systems in the United States developed can inform planning for future health-care processes and payment systems. Studying the history leading to the current situation in American health care may enable better decisions for individualizing preventive and health maintenance care. That is, examining the development of American health care may illuminate the role of the doctor-patient relationship within the business of health care. Seeking focused medical decisions through the lens of the doctor-patient relationship can bring to fruition meaningful and efficient use of resources for both health maintenance patients and chronic disease patients while simultaneously providing a method for compassionate help at the end of life.

— THREE —

The Way We Were

The interactions between physician, patient, and payer (or the government) developed from ancient roots which may help us understand the modern quandary concerning cost, quality, and personalization in medical care. As occurs today, ancient health-care providers followed certain "schools of thought" and, often, protocols. Patients with wealth were more likely to access personalized health care while others either received the equivalent of first aid or state-supported care based on an algorithm. Payers who were wealthy paid with cash equivalents, state and groups utilized a tax system including the temple tax, and some individuals bartered for services.

In the ancient days, the roles of each participant in health care may have been more clearly defined because care was mostly given for acute needs. In contrast, chronic diseases usually led to early death or inconsequential life. The latter is illustrated by the lives of Uzziah, who was considered a good ruler until he was struck with leprosy leading to his removal from public life described in 2 Chronicles 26:1-23, and of King Baldwin IV of Jerusalem, who developed leprosy at puberty and died in 1185 as a young man having accomplished little before relinquishing ruling power.[61] Ancient care for chronic disease often consisted of segregation such as leper colonies. Some patients sought medical care by pilgrimage, bearing a costly offering, to temples and oracles in hopes of receiving a miracle cure. Established hospitals and sanitariums were not part of the ancient world. Eventually sanitariums were developed as a public health measure of quarantine and care but not until 1854 in Germany to combat tuberculosis.[62] Physician shopping also occurred in the ancient past, as seen by the woman with a bleeding discharge described by the ancient physician Luke in Luke 8:41-48. That woman sought care from many physicians without improving her chronic disease. Moreover, recovery from a chronic disease depended on the innate healing ability of the human body rather than on curative measures given or done to a patient.

In these early years of medicine, acute care for diseases or injuries concentrated on symptom relief and mechanical support. Herbalists made medicinal teas and poultices, which would be available to anyone who could make a payment or find ingredients. The wealthy also had access to public therapies, such as hot mineral baths. In view of the value of well-trained soldiers,

Figure 2. "Medicine and Surgery," Crystalinks.com

battlefield injuries stimulated the development of acute injury care and, consequently, the training of physicians including surgical specialists. The mural entitled "Soldier and Physician," found in Pompeii, depicts surgical removal of an arrow from a Roman soldier by a battlefield medic.[63] Medical care was focused mainly on acute medical and surgical problems.

Physicians could be found in wealthy households usually as indentured servants or slaves. The expense of education, room, and board was paid by the very wealthy. Repayment for the cost for training, perhaps like repayment of medical education debt, was usually over a lifetime of indentured service or slavery. However, the physician was not necessarily confined to a single location if the biblical physician Luke was a physician-slave. Thus, this form of the employee-physician model is ancient but was used only by very wealthy patients. It is notable that Galen was an exception to the slave rule as his wealthy father paid for training in the school of Asclepius while he remained a free citizen.[64] Because physicians were frequently obligated to wealthy households, actual use of physicians and physician-prescribed therapeutic services was not circumscribed by economic factors to the degree found today. Affording ownership of a physician meant affording the cost of medical care.

On the other hand, care for the peasant classes came partly from midwives and herbalists who learned the trade by apprenticeship. Herodotus, the Greek historian, described the care as rendering nonprofessional advice: "They bring out all their sick into the streets, for they have no regular doctors. People that come along offer the sick man advice, either from what they personally have found to cure such a complaint, or what they have known someone else to be cured by. No one is allowed to pass by a sick person without asking him what ails him."[65]

Medical care was individualized but limited in scope as it was usually administered as the equivalent of a house call carrying the pharmacy. While the economic model was not prepaid concierge or capitation in nature, these providers sometimes received local support to stay in an area in the form of temple taxes. Temple priests offered algorithmic medical instructions to the non-slave classes in some societies, especially exemplified by the Hebrews following Mosaic Law. After successful therapy, these temples superimposed a fee-for-service payment model in the form of mandated temple sacrifices. However, for most members of the poorer classes, medical care consisted of first aid and hope for recovery.

Individualized patient care was not the usual focus for providing remedies centuries ago. In these ancient times, medical therapeutic decisions were algorithmic in nature, partly because of a lack of therapeutic options and partly because of the infrequency of long-term survival providing knowledge about chronic diseases. Algorithms were developed in the setting of traditional approaches to disease and often reflected the rudimentary nature of science regarding physiology and pathophysiology. In contrast, the Greek school of Pythagoras tried to systematize medical care. The Pythagorean school supported an approach emphasizing the application of number theory to medical care,[66] in which health was ascribed to natural cycles associated with the numbers four, seven, and their product, twenty-eight.[67] Numerology was used to predict favorable personality characteristics to be emulated leading to better health. Apparently, vegetarianism was an important component of Pythagorean health, too.[68] Failure of therapy was ascribed to supernatural factors.[69] Also prevalent in Asian cultures was the dualism of Chinese medical care emphasizing yin-yang harmony for restoring health from disease states using meditation and exercises. However, Chinese medicine did personalize care through physical exam and inoculation as described in the *Handbook of Prescriptions for Emergency Treatments* published before the year 341.[70] Harmony, for the Chinese patient, was restored by diet changes and mechanical processes including massage, acupuncture, and breathing exercises.[71] However, innovative medical practice was not part of the thinking about patient care in any of these health-care thought processes as the results were deemed less important than the process although payments were sometimes linked to survival.[72] Such attitudes carried forward hundreds of years as seen in the use of leeches and bloodletting in Revolutionary War-era American medicine influenced by Benjamin Rush,[73] who is known as the Father of American Medicine. A famous example of algorithm-influenced medical care occurred at the death of George Washington from a severe throat infection (epiglottis) obstructing his breathing. His physician team, led by Dr. James

Craik, prescribed bloodletting (five pints of blood), poultices, and rectal administration of medicines while dismissing use of the new procedure of tracheostomy. Tracheostomy would have prolonged his life but not treated the infection.[74] In this example, the usual medical thinking from ancient times was one therapy remained good for many diseases and patients.

In contrast, the Onidian School and Hippocrates pioneered other approaches. As the first Greek medical school, the Onidian School viewed each disease and each organ as isolated or unrelated to the rest of the body. Medical care focused only on the organ identified as diseased, analogous in some ways to subspecialty medical care found today. Conversely, Hippocrates[75] established a school of medicine before 400 B.C.E. on the Island of Kos, off the coast of modern Turkey, in response to the Onidian or Cnidian School. Hippocrates thought that a patient should be viewed wholly, made up of many organs. Hippocrates advanced the concept of individualized medical care by making it a holistic approach to the patient as outlined in his famous oath:

> I swear by Apollo the Healer, by Asclepius, by Hygieia, by Panacea, and by all the gods and goddesses, making them my witnesses, that I will carry out, according to my ability and judgment, this oath and this indenture.
>
> To hold my teacher in this art equal to my own parents; to make him partner in my livelihood; when he is in need of money to share mine with him; to consider his family as my own brothers, and to teach them this art, if they want to learn it, without fee or indenture; to impart precept, oral instruction, and all other instruction to my own sons, the sons of my teacher, and to indentured pupils who have taken the physician's oath, but to nobody else.
>
> I will use treatment to help the sick according to my ability and judgment, but never with a view to injury and

wrong-doing. Neither will I administer a poison to anybody when asked to do so, nor will I suggest such a course. Similarly I will not give to a woman a pessary to cause abortion. But I will keep pure and holy both my life and my art. I will not use the knife, not even, verily, on sufferers from stone, but I will give place to such as are craftsmen therein.

Into whatsoever houses I enter, I will enter to help the sick, and I will abstain from all intentional wrong-doing and harm, especially from abusing the bodies of man or woman, bond or free. And whatsoever I shall see or hear in the course of my profession, as well as outside my profession in my intercourse with men, if it be what should not be published abroad, I will never divulge, holding such things to be holy secrets.

Now if I carry out this oath, and break it not, may I gain for ever reputation among all men for my life and for my art; but if I transgress it and forswear myself, may the opposite befall me. (Translation by W. H. S. Jones)[76]

The modern interpretation of the Hippocratic Oath has been "first do no harm." This approach acknowledged the necessity to provide care based on the individual doctor-patient relationship in which benefit or harm from medical care depended on the patient context. Recognizing and granting value for individualizing care of the individual patient are inherent in the process of providing care that benefits rather than harms health. The import of the Hippocratic Oath is not that harm or mistakes never occur but that the close attention and compassionate intention of the physician must guide therapy for the best possible outcome.

The Hippocratic Oath was first used by modern medical schools in 1508 at the University of Wittenberg, followed in 1804 at the medical school in Montpellier, France. In the eighteenth century, Hippocrates was not formally acknowledged but influenced the ideal of individualized medical care and professional duty to the patient espoused by John Gregory and Thomas Percival. Gregory's *Lectures on the Duties and Qualifications of a Physician*, published in 1772, reflected "the central tenet of Scottish moral sense theory, that morality is a function, not of actions and their consequences, but of motivation and character."[77] Gregory and Percival, influenced by Hippocrates, in turn influenced the transformation of British, and therefore western, medical care from being a trade of barbers to a professional art imbued with compassion for the patient.[78]

The formal use of the Hippocratic Oath in American medical schools occurred about 20 percent of the time throughout much of the twentieth century.[79] In 1993, 55 percent of the medical graduations involved administering an oath with components that can be traced back to the Hippocratic Oath.[80] Edmund Pellegrino avers that the lineage of medical responsibility derived from the Hippocratic Oath makes health-care providers a moral community rather than a guild or business.[81] The importance of the individualized care and the doctor-patient relationship was reinforced by these uses of these oaths by the American medical community and training institutions.

Despite these changes in motivation and training for the practice of medicine, the ability of practitioners to provide individualized or community-based medical care remained bound to the payment system. The payment system for medical care changed as the world moved away from the feudal system of the few wealthy owners contrasted with slave and indentured classes. Development of a middle class led to free individuals who practiced medicine as a livelihood which became a profession. Fee-for-service was promoted early in the history of American health care establishing a price structure for a gainful wage while ensuring integrity of the profession. A fee-bill, for example, was endorsed by a group of physicians who used the technique to exclude untrained or otherwise deemed unworthy individuals from practice as seen in the photograph of a fee-bill from 1848. Payments at that time remained fee-for-service covering acute care.

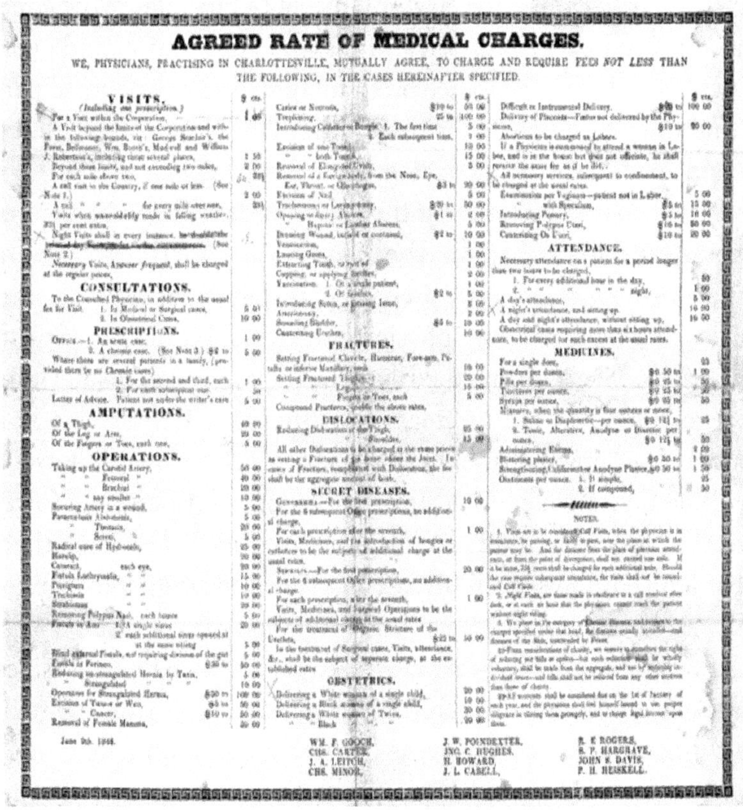
AGREED RATE OF MEDICAL CHARGES.

WE, PHYSICIANS, PRACTISING IN CHARLOTTESVILLE, MUTUALLY AGREE, TO CHARGE AND REQUIRE FEES *NOT LESS* THAN THE FOLLOWING, IN THE CASES HEREINAFTER SPECIFIED.

VISITS.

CONSULTATIONS.

PRESCRIPTIONS.

AMPUTATIONS.

OPERATIONS.

FRACTURES.

DISLOCATIONS.

SECRET DISEASES.

OBSTETRICS.

ATTENDANCE.

MEDICINES.

NOTES.

WM. F. GOOCH,
CHS. CARTER,
J. A. LEITCH,
CHS. MINOR,

J. W. POINDEXTER,
JNO. C. HUGHES,
H. HOWARD,
J. L. CABELL,

R. E. ROGERS,
S. P. HARGRAVE,
JOHN S. DAVIS,
P. H. HEISKELL.

Figure 3. Agreed Rate of Medical Charges, 1848. Historical Collections and Services, The Claude Moore Health Sciences Library, University of Virginia.

Health insurance plans were available for fee-for-service but were mostly used to pay for accident-related care until 1847. That year, the Massachusetts Health Insurance Company of Boston offered a group insurance plan with comprehensive benefits based on fee-for-service physician payments.[82] However, that insurance plan remained a local phenomenon.

Universally available changes in payment systems through health insurance did not occur until the twentieth century when prepaid hospitalization was offered by hospitals. In Texas, a program started in 1929, mostly for Dallas, Texas, schoolteachers, provided twenty-one days of prepaid care in the Baylor University Hospital.[83] The concept was embraced by the American Hospital Association and evolved into the Blue Cross insurance program directing payments to participating hospitals, especially after 1939.[84] A similar concept led to a prepaid insurance for physician services to loggers and miners in the Pacific Northwest during the early 1900s.[85] To avoid becoming hospital employees under the Blue Cross insurance program, physicians countered with prepaid plans analogous to the Pacific Northwest model covering physician services. This insurance plan for physician services became the Blue Shield program in 1946.[86] Joining the two programs led to creation of the Blue Cross/Blue Shield Insurance Company. Other health insurance companies followed the new Blue Cross/Blue Shield Insurance Company pattern. However, covering costs as an individual health-care encounter rather than an individualized long-term disease management remained the focus of the payment system.

After World War II, Congress froze wages, which forced businesses to attract employees by offering fringe benefits. Thus, providing health insurance for employees became a common fringe benefit. Demand for health care facility-based services increased as benefits increased covering medical care. Availability of health-care facilities was increased by passage of the Hospital Survey and Construction Act of 1946, known as the Hill-Burton Law. Although considered by Congress as a jobs program, federal funding for building these new facilities (over 6,800 built by 2000)[87] increased the usefulness of medical insurance which remunerated hospital-based medical costs. As a result, more sites for hospital-based care accumulated as funding for care at those sites became common.

Insurance coverage increased to about 60 percent of the population during the 1950s, supported by the Revenue Act of 1954 that made insurance costs a deductible business expense.[88] However, insurance coverage continued to be mostly used for hospital services as 67 percent of the expenditures in 1965.[89] Moreover, the elderly, retired, unemployed, and under-employed population paid for medical care directly, without health insurance, or remained undertreated leading to the 1965 passage of the Social Security Act Amendments creating Medicare (Title XVIII) and Medicaid (Title XIX). The emphasis of this legislation was coverage for hospital and surgical expenses while ignoring the transformation of American medical care focus from acute disease to chronic disease. This deficiency was observed by Rosemary Stevens:

> It was quite possible in the early 1960s to anticipate the changing focus in epidemiology from acute to chronic disease that we are grappling with today. However, from the perspective of the 1960s, the advantage of conceiving of chronic diseases as treatable along the same lines as acute conditions meant that the U.S. system of health services and health insurance (premised, as it was, on cure rather than on care of long-term, continuing sickness) need not be tampered with to fit the changing patterns of disease. Put a different way, if heart disease, cancer, and stroke could be "fixed," then the aggressive style of American medicine-science-based, disease-focused, technological, and interventionist might be justified as a primary basis for national health policy in the future, as it had, successfully, in earlier decades without radical changes in the system.[90]

As health-care costs rose from $41.9 billion in 1965 to $92.7 billion in 1972,[91] an attempt to control the payment system was enacted by the Congress through the Health Maintenance Organization Act of 1973 (HMO Act). Based on six health maintenance organizations

(HMOs) established from 1929 through 1947, the law's provisions were for "basic health services," acute-care services, and outpatient "mental health services (not to exceed 20 visits)."[92] Cost containment and savings were the goal of HMOs, using primary care physicians as gatekeepers. Medical care expenditures authorized by gatekeeping physicians were tied to financial incentives for those physicians.[93] The increasing need for chronic disease management was not considered by Congress in the initial establishment of HMOs. The regulations pertaining to the HMO Act did not address patient preferences regarding health care decisions, leading to patient dissatisfaction. By the mid-1980s, patient dissatisfaction with HMOs worsened, reflecting the plan's inherent limitation of health-care choices and reduction in patient participation with the health-care decision process. To address consumer complaints about restricted medical care, HMOs evolved into the managed care organization (MCO). The MCO model improved patient satisfaction by increasing easy access to specialty care as well as promoting personalized care by primary physicians.[94] However, the MCO remained a variation of the HMO structure.

Further evolution of health service payment systems led to development of two more insurance plans other than the restrictive and inflexible HMO or MCO types. Point-of-service (POS) plans are based on using a network of providers, charging patients co-payments for most services while using a gatekeeper primary care physician. By charging patients, POS plans attempted to control patient utilization of services through required deductible payments and per-visit co-payments by the patient.[95] The POS plan developed as a mildly less expensive and more flexible insurance policy compared to the HMO. However, total cost for health care increased annually through higher premium charges and increasing amounts for deductible and visit payments.

Another kind of health insurance, preferred provider organizations (PPO), attempts to control costs by using networks of contracted services. The insurance companies and policy regulators assume health-care providers will elect to have an assured patient population in return for discounting fees for services. The PPO became the most popular insurance plan by reducing patient premiums while pre-authorizing requirements for referrals to specialist physicians. However, PPO plans have created confusion about in-network and out-of-network status for rendered services. Medical services can be rendered before the network status of the provider is clarified, leading to surprise billing to the patient.

These health insurance plans attempted to lower health-care costs by reducing payments to providers in addition to increasing patient-borne costs. Physician fees are contracted by most payers except Medicare, which publishes a fee schedule annually. These Medicare fee schedules for physicians are based on the intensity of rendered service, the location of service, and a committee-determined relative value for the service.[96] As the Medicare beneficiary population has grown, the Medicare fee schedule has been accepted to be the market value for services. Commercial health insurance companies use the Medicare fee schedule as a basis for contracting physician and physician groups. Usually physicians agreed to a percentage of Medicare fee in exchange for inclusion in that insurance network of physicians. Thus, inflation in physician fees remained constrained by Medicare decisions and contracts for participation with commercial health-insurance customers. However, total physician payment has continued to rise regardless of changes in the fee schedules.

Failure to reverse growth in the physician component of health-care expenditures reflects increased demand for services linked to the growing number of recipients needing long-term health care. However, the attempt to reduce the physician component of health-care cost by reducing payment for individual services affects the supply of physicians meeting increased demand for health-care services. Enlisting physicians through solicited contracts or voluntary enrollment assumes a willingness of physicians to participate in the government-regulated health-care system. That is, physicians are assumed to be constrained by involvement in a doctor-patient relationship. Such an assumption fails under scrutiny. For instance, only 52 percent of American physicians plan to continue their current practice with about 45 percent planning to reduce hours or retire. About 15 percent of polled physicians plan to decline future participation in Medicare and Medicaid plans.[97] Some physicians plan to provide services for an amount of cash unrelated to the Medicare fee schedule. Other potential physicians decide to follow a different career path unrelated to medical care. Coupled with an insufficient number of physicians in training and physicians leaving practice, a shortfall up to 121,900 total physicians is projected for the year 2032.[98] None of the legislative attempts to reduce health-care costs examined the effect of laws on the willingness for physicians to participate in the insurance plan nor the effect on point-of-service quality of care for the patient and the doctor-patient relationship.

Health insurance plan formulations and unacknowledged physician supply problems negatively impact attempts to implement Rosemary Stevens's call to treat chronic disease differently than acute disease. Treating chronic disease requires enlarging the number of health-care workers involved. Paying for chronic disease treatment requires changing definitions of service and rules for reimbursement to the chronic disease management model. However, changing to such a model has not occurred as seen with the first chronic disease specifically covered by Medicare disability status, kidney failure.

Chronic disease management in kidney failure has not been a financially defined concept of care as payment remained based on fee-for-service. The financial concept is illustrated by the payment method for End-Stage Kidney Disease (ESRD) mandated by the Social Security Amendments Act of 1972.[99] Nephrologist services supervising dialysis for ESRD patients received a monthly remuneration from Medicare that was years later modified to be based on the number of physician-patient encounters during that month. While the time period was a month, the payment was basically fee-for-service. Notably, the first payments to nephrologists were routed through the dialysis clinic ownership as part of a lump sum dialysis services payment. Physician complaints led to separation of the physician fee from the dialysis facility fee. Thus, initial recognition that dialysis requires team management of a chronic disease was unintentionally subverted by the fee-for-service system separately paying corporate and physician components of the management team.

Recognition of the need for long-term disease management appeared to happen within private HMOs like Kaiser-Permanente as a part of general health maintenance,[100] but most calls for chronic disease care occurred without recognizing a need to change the payment system from the usual fee-for-service method. Payer reasoning remained that medical care is an acute care service.[101] The political, social, and health-care system focus remained on providing payment plans for patient access to acute medical treatment rather than on long-term disease management. As consequence of rendering more services to more people, total costs increased.

To control government costs, legislation attempted to transfer insurance premium responsibility from the government to the private sector. Corporate tax-deductible self-insurance by private businesses was encouraged with the Employee Retirement Income Security Act of 1974, but the fee-for-service payment plan continued to be followed.[102] However, despite these laws, hospital use and associated medical costs continued to rise. An attempt to control rising hospital costs on a fee-for-service basis led to passage of the Tax Equity and Fiscal Responsibility Act of 1982 mandating development of a diagnosis-related group (DRG) payment system.[103] The DRG was intended for Medicare beneficiaries as a "prospective payment system" for hospitalizations. An entire hospital stay was treated as a single service. The law was projected to stem the rising health-care costs by saving 3 to 4 billion dollars over three years.[104] Instead, from 1983 to 1986, health-care spending rose from $367.8 billion to $474.7 billion.[105] Another attempt to reduce government health-care spending was made with the Balanced Budget Act of 1997, which anticipated reducing medical spending $127 billion over four years by reducing payments to hospitals and providers while increasing Medicare beneficiary deductible payments to $1,500. Instead, total health care spending increased from $1.202 trillion in 1998 to $1.6292 trillion in 2002,[106] much of it for Medicare beneficiaries. Legislated control over health-care spending continued to produce a contrarian effect on health-care costs.

While spending on hospital services remained the major component of health-care expenditures, recognition of the contribution by the pharmaceutical industry to the rising national health-care bill arose by the year 2000. Pharmaceutical costs were noted to have increased three times faster than general inflation and two times faster than medical care cost inflation from 1998 to 2000.[107] A report by the National Center for Policy Analysis attributed drug cost increases to governmental "mal-regulation" of procurement and dispensing processes for medications.[108] Thus, medication supply remained inadequate to meet demand. In the Harvard Health Blog, Ameet Sarpatwari attributed the increased drug costs to insufficient generic drug production based on inadequate competition.[109] That is, federal regulations inhibited growth and competition in the pharmaceutical manufacturing industry, which restricted medication supply capacity. Supply and demand economics led to higher drug prices worsened by monopolistic control of individually prescribed drug production.

Lack of competition reflected a low number of licensed manufacturers, lapses in production due to safety issues, and delayed Food and Drug Administration (FDA) approval of generic manufacturing plants. The FDA application time was forty-two months for generic drugs versus eight months for new drugs.[110] The limited number of pharmaceutical production facilities, as pointed out by

Sarpatwari's blog, is the most vulnerable component affecting drug costs. Decreased production of generic drug stocks increased costs by forcing use of higher priced substitute medications. Loss of a manufacturing plant due to Food and Drug Administration action or natural disaster became a reality in 2017. This vulnerability in pharmaceutical manufacturing was magnified by Hurricane Maria's effect of stopping pharmaceutical manufacturing in Puerto Rico.[111]

Congress legislated a voluntary insurance plan to pay the increasing costs of medication. Drug cost for the elderly and disabled population was addressed by enactment of a Medicare insurance program through the Medicare Modernization Act of 2003 (MMA 2003) using a lump-sum approach for payments.[112] The law was flawed in that the lump-sum payment rules created a gap in covered costs, known as the "doughnut hole," before catastrophic insurance coverage for medications began. Notably, the law failed to address the cost for individual medications, treating a pharmacy bill as a single drug regardless of the number of medications prescribed. A co-dependent financial effect increasing individual drug costs was generated by the MMA 2003 payment system. The increased availability of money for medication was followed by suppliers' increasing the drug prices. A medication cost would be paid until the lump-sum limit was reached. Thus, MMA 2003 unintentionally incentivized price increases for drugs. Costs for pharmaceuticals continued to rise despite federal governmental efforts to the contrary.

Consequently, failure to control these increasing costs for American health care led to a different approach to increase health insurance participation via the Patient Protection and Affordable Care Act (ACA) signed into law in 2010.[113] This law reflected a change to coerced health-insurance purchasing. Although taxes supporting Medicare are collected as part of federal income tax, participation in Medicare involved choice and was not available to most Americans under the age of 65. Pharmaceutical insurance participation by Medicare beneficiaries was also voluntary as provided by the MMA

2003.[114] ACA-mandated coerced participation in health insurance expanded from Medicare and Medicaid beneficiaries to the whole population of the United States. Both the MMA 2003 and ACA failed to encourage marketplace competitive forces for controlling costs, which contributed to the rise in health-care-related prices following enactment of these laws. The MMA 2003, for example, prohibited "interference" by Medicare and Medicaid administrations with private competition that affected drug prices, thus excluding those government insurance beneficiaries from lower drug costs associated with competitive bidding.[115] With a similar effect, the ACA restricted insurance plan design while imposing increased financial risk to insurance underwriters that failed to fully implement those designs. ACA rules stipulated that health exchange insurance policies achieve goals published annually by the secretary of Health and Human Services or pay costly nonperformance penalties. As an effect of the liability imposed by ACA, fewer insurance companies chose to participate in the federally designed health exchanges, thus reducing competition in that health insurance marketplace. The number of health insurance companies participating in the health insurance market also fell because business conditions subsequent to passage of ACA were conducive to health insurance company mergers. Thus, the number of health insurance companies willing to offer health exchange insurance plans decreased.[116]

In summation, these developmental influences on American health care payment methods continued a fee-for-service mentality paying for the medical care for a growing population. Health insurance became the main payer for medical services during the twentieth century. As the population increased and aged, need for medical care increased so that costs for medical care soared despite attempts to lower total payments. These endeavors include use of gatekeeper physicians to reduce referrals and procedures, network formation to reduce the number of participating physicians, financial risk shifting to influence physician and patient behavior, and refusal to approve payment for selected medications and procedures. Other efforts have reduced direct payments for services by the federal government insurance programs while assuming health care providers would accept reduced pay rather than stop seeing patients. These dominant forces in health care economics failed to consider the individual patient who prefers personalized health decisions. Also, the government and business regulations fail to acknowledge how health decisions are best made within the doctor-patient relationship. Furthermore, there is a general failure to recognize the transformation of acute disease states to chronic disease states, which requires a change to chronic disease management and financing.

FOUR

The Way We Are as an Industry

odern efforts to increase the quality and quantity of health-care services eventually led to a change from a doctor-patient relationship to a provider-payer-patient relationship. This intercalation into the doctor-patient relationship has accelerated as prolonged and innovative medical care becomes more expensive. Medical care also became more complicated necessitating building new facilities and research laboratories. Payment under the ancient barter negotiation system would allow a provider to offer needed services for cash or food but would not finance either building a hospital or developing innovative treatment options. Demand for medical services also increased when American businesses wanted a healthy workforce[117] while, simultaneously, American society embraced the concept of equal access to developments in medical therapy regardless of cost. Indeed, medical care is now being called an American right[118] rather than a person's need. An additional factor to consider, the number of persons over sixty-five years in age, requiring more health services, rose from 1.7 million in 1880 to 34.9 million in 2000.[119] As supply of therapies, demand for services, and costs for innovation increase, supply and cost for services demonstrate co-dependent rather than a balanced effect on costs. That is, all costs increase.

Wellness, as an unexpected example, has also become more expensive as seen in the cost for vaccinations such as the Human Papilloma Virus vaccine. This vaccine, which is subject to societal controversy, costs $390 to $500 for each of three injections with variable coverage by health insurance companies.[120] Vaccinations are now available for multiple chronic diseases, which increases total expenditures for such health maintenance therapy. Costs for vaccines include money allocated to cover actual or potential class-action lawsuits filed when adverse effects from vaccination occur. Besides vaccinations, screening for disease has become part of health maintenance including imaging for cancer, imaging for artery disease, procedures looking for colon cancer, and others. The aging population desires wellness, and that population continues to grow in number. Indeed, Medicare, for example, requires documentation of health maintenance and disease screening services for payments to primary care physicians. An increasing number of patients requiring chronic health maintenance, such as vaccinations and cancer screens, increases total expenditures for wellness.

An infrequently considered factor is the effect of successful therapy on the expense for provision of medical care. For seniors over sixty years of age, living from 1980 to 2014, life expectancy in the United States increased by five years.[121] The number of people retiring, living longer, and, therefore, likely to use health-care services, continues to increase. As an example, federal government civil service retirements almost doubled from 2000 to 2013.[122] Resulting medical care expenditures are increasing as a larger volume of services are offered to a burgeoning population of older health-care recipients. Increasing complexity of the health-care service needed for more senior people with chronic disease multiplies the costs as well. We have become a country of older people living with one or more complex diseases.

Consequently, private insurance and governmental payers for health care services necessarily seek to control cost by inserting the payer between the provider and the patient. Self-pay patients, by contrast, control costs by reducing visits to doctors, negotiating prices, or choosing low-cost therapy.[123] The third-party payer intrusion into the doctor-patient relationship occurs during attempts of third-party payers to control costs. That intrusion can produce a co-dependent supply-demand, cost-control, incremental-service mentality affecting medical cost by using more services. Frequently unrecognized is the management expense necessary to monitor health-care expenditures while formulating algorithms and policies for those expenditures. That is, people are hired to be overseers of the health-care payment system, which consumes part of the health-care dollar.

The cost-control approach frequently uses an algorithm which may delay use of the definitive procedure. Algorithms, by design, force a step-by-step process from initial evaluation to completion of final therapy. Subsequently, demand is increased for all services required by the algorithm. An example in service delay occurs when a patient with a severely symptomatic, acutely and severely herniated vertebral disk is forced to undergo exercise therapy, use of potentially addicting pain medications, and have multiple doctor office visits before back surgery is allowed. Incremental services and pain medication use often increase costs if definitive surgery is delayed. Meanwhile, the patient risks opioid dependency and loss of functionality in the workplace or at home. Allowing direct access to definitive therapy may reduce both time for healing and complications for the patient.

Also affecting the industry, growth in provider-ordered services may reflect the desire to provide the "latest and greatest" therapy. As an unintended consequence, the presence of third-party payments has increased demand for more and costlier services and medications. This situation is analogous to the impact of student loans and scholarships on the cost of higher education.[124] Wolfram's analysis of college costs suggested a direct correlation between increasing government funding as a third-party payer and rises in student tuition. Similarly, when payment is made by a third party, consideration of costs tends not to be made by the physician and patient or the patient's family. Instead, a "do-everything" mentality regardless of cost may develop because insurance money is available to pay.

A "do-everything" mentality may include early use of the latest therapies. Provision of new therapies is usually expensive as seen in the price of newly prescribed cancer treatments that are projected to rise about 27 percent from 2010 to 2020.[125] Demand for the new treatments feeds the increase in cost. Patient demand for such services has increased without necessarily weighing curative and restorative likelihood of various treatment options. This demand is enhanced by pharmaceutical advertisements on television. Television advertising, which began May 19, 1983, was aimed at increasing patient demand for more medications. An example is the advertisement for Vioxx by Merck beginning in 1999. Using an international figure skating star as spokesperson, the sales of that drug increased to $2,500,000,000 over the five years after advertising began. However, the medication was withdrawn from market after field reports of severe side effects accumulated.[126] PEW Research found that the "do everything, doctor" mantra has increased from 15 percent to 31 percent of poll respondents from 1990 to 2013.[127] The costs for providing the latest therapy that "does everything" includes the research expense to bring a new drug to market. Adams and Brantner, who worked for the Federal Trade Commission, averred that the cost for developing a new drug was minimally $800,000,000.[128] Accruing multiple new pharmaceutical agents becomes expense as illustrated with the price for drugs treating cancer costing $32.6 billion in 2014 with the average monthly cost of newer cancer treatments being $10,000.[129] Medical progress is often seen by patients and providers as using the latest innovation and medication regardless of a high cost or likely effectiveness.

The response of payers to these cost increases, which are stimulated by factors outside of payer control, has focused on disrupting the ease of obtaining services or benefits. Ostensibly, the reasoning for restraining delivery of therapies focuses on complying with "evidence-based medicine." Attempts to reduce the cost of pharmaceuticals have led to institutionalization of preferred drug lists, prior authorization policies, and arrangements for monetary rebates from companies to providers based on medication choice,[130] without any consideration for the clinical impact on individual patient care. Controlling medication utilization may occur through requirements of pre-authorization and post-facto denials of payment, but both techniques utilize single-event processes that have less predictable benefit for the ongoing care of the patient while risking harm to the patient through interrupting therapeutic processes. That is, controlling costs through delaying implementation of a therapy may lead to therapeutic failure for the patient who dies or becomes incapable of taking the medication while awaiting authorization for therapy.

A nonfatal example is the denial of payment by Blue Cross Health Insurance Company for Dexilant given to a patient with reflux-induced Barrett's esophagus. Barrett's esophagus is known to be a precancerous condition. Despite failure of multiple medication regimens to treat this precancerous disease, coupled with a biopsy-demonstrated resolution of the Barrett's esophagus when Dexilant was used, payment for that drug was neither covered nor applied to health insurance deductible costs despite multiple appeals to the health insurance company.[131]

Another developing approach to control costs involves real-time control of diagnostic test utilization. A system to approve magnetic resonance imaging (MRI) use at the time the test is ordered is being developed in Spain and Portugal.[132] The real-time control process allows a discussion about the use of the MRI as the test request is made, which may allow a more effective use of the technology. In contrast, cost control of medical services by payers in the United States usually proceeds through a payer-controlled, truncated view based on population statistics regarding the ordered care. The decision about payment for a service is not made at the time service is needed through discussion between the doctor, patient, and payer representative. Instead, the service is delayed or refused until an unknown reviewer decides about authorization. Sometimes the completed service is subsequently denied payment, especially when the service is part of urgent or emergency care. The decision about payment is not made with the patient nor necessarily involves the long-term plan of care for the patient.

Passage of the Patient Care and Affordable Care Act (ACA) in 2010 was purported to solve the problem about provision of health care to the American populace. The act mandated purchasing insurance coverage for each person while also mandating coverage provisions for all health insurance policies.[133] Apparently, Congress hoped the one-size-fits-all format would both attract more enrollees and dilute the cost per covered person. Controlling the format of health insurance would then lead to controlling the rising cost of health care. However, semantics are involved in the congressional assessment of the law. According to Robert Farley on FactCheck. org, Rep. Chris Van Hollen as ranking Democrat of the House Budget Committee stated that the ACA "has resulted in significantly reducing the per capita cost of health care," when interviewed on MSNBC February 12, 2014. On enquiry for clarification, Mr. Van Hollen's office stated, "he meant that the ACA has significantly *reduced the growth* in health care costs."[134] Thus, the congressional goal with passing ACA seems to have been slowing the rise in health care costs by creating a truncated or single-payer system without incurring more beneficiary costs. However, costs of health care have continued to rise to an estimated 22 percent of gross domestic product in 2017.[135] Costs paid by the patient are part of this rise in total expenditures in the form of higher premiums and higher deductibles.[136]

Organized medicine[137] and academic think-tanks[138] viewed the Affordable Care Act as the dual solution to pay for uncompensated medical care and to remove uncertainty about the revenue stream for health-care providers and businesses. However, an unintended effect of the Affordable Care Act has been to reduce the number of participating physicians in health exchanges as the number of participating insurance companies falls, thereby reducing the number of health exchanges with their physician panels. Payments also are sometimes reduced from usual amounts to physicians who participate in a specific health exchange network or belong to a narrow network within a health exchange.[139] Coupled with increasing premiums, which averaged 23.4 percent in 2017, a decreasing number of partic- ipating physicians and a decreasing availability of participating insurers limiting 57 percent of enrollees to three or fewer insurers offering a health-insurance product, Mark Bertolini, CEO of Aetna, Inc, stated that "Obamacare" is entering a "death spiral."[140] This effect of the Affordable Care Act on premiums and availability also reflects the 2017 expiration of "risk corridors" and "re-insurance" government subsidies for health exchange insurers, with these terminations decreasing the profit margin for insurers.[141] A further effect of the Affordable Care Act on premiums and availability occurs because of government mandates about scope of coverage and exclusions by all health insurance companies as illustrated by the HealthCare. gov website for choosing an ACA plan.[142] These regulations force participating patients and insurers to choose from a-few-sizes-fit-all policies. With fewer product choices, premiums and deductible limits are unrestrained by competitive forces. Furthermore, the ACA has influenced all health insurance policies. According to Xtelligent Healthcare Media, LLC, "One of the most significant impacts of the landmark legislation is the upward trajectory of premiums, deductibles, and out-of-pocket costs, especially with plans sold on the health insurance exchanges."[143] Thus, worker annual health-care premiums for family coverage rose 80 percent to $16,351 from 2003 to 2013.[144] Annual deductible limits averaged $6,000 in 2015, according to Paul Ketchel of the Daily News,[145] which is an increase of 67 percent in five years.[146] Such high deductible costs disproportionately influence lower-income patients, who being unable to afford health insurance, decide to postpone or forego health care. The effect is adverse for maintaining revenue for the health-care businesses and maintaining health of patients.

As an illustration, the effect on individual health insurance costs is shown by the decisions of a kidney transplant patient who is the owner of a small business. In 2018, the monthly premium for this patient was increased from about $1,100 a month to more than $2,000 a month with a $10,000 deductible payment annually. The patient dropped the health insurance policy without finding a replacement as he expected post-transplant care would cost less than the $34,000 personal expense mandated by the insurance company.[147] Another illustration of the personal monetary cost of medical care is the increasing use of the emergency room as the place of primary patient care, according to the American College of Emergency Physicians.[148] As emergency rooms are legally required to see all patients, medical care can be obtained without first paying the co-pay amount or deductible amount of money. When these effects are combined with the more than twenty-five changes to the federal tax code affecting patients, providers, and health-care businesses,[149] medical care and payment responsibilities for moderate income patients, medical businesses and the health insurance industry have become confused, chaotic, and less predictable. Uncertainty about these effects has increased with the passage of the Tax Cuts and Jobs Act of 2017 repealing the tax penalty for individuals failing to obtain health insurance in 2019 but not the mandate to have health insurance. Other congressional bills to repeal or change the ACA law have not gained traction for passage. Thus, the Affordable Care

Act continues to directly influence American health care unless it is repealed.

Chaotic medical business economics have affected the physician practice style, as well. Private practice physicians face increasing economic pressures from overhead costs. Primary care physicians have overhead costs of 59.5 percent of revenue or more.[150] Likewise, specialists have more difficulty paying the overhead for an office practice since they need to remain in the hospital for provision of patient care.[151] Costs to implement federally mandated electronic medical records required by the HITECH Act of 2009 add to the overhead, disproportionately affecting solo practitioners by an average cost of $163,765 compared to $233,298 for a five-physician practice.[152] These hard costs for electronic record systems do not account for "soft" costs from decreased productivity reflecting increased time needed for electronic medical record completion which, in turn, reduces time to see patients. For example, in the relatively uniform and controlled environment at Lehigh Valley Health Network, obstetrician productivity fell 45-49 percent with implementation of electronic records. Recovery of productivity to baseline levels at Lehigh Valley Health Network took four years.[153] To increase a provider's productivity defined as face-to-face time with patients, nonphysician providers are hired as scribes, technical support personnel, billing support and services personnel, data security experts, and government compliance officers. These additional nonphysician employees address government mandated privacy issues, meaningful use compliance issues, and data reporting leading to the future pay-for-performance, while not directly generating revenue. Seeking to increase meaningful and billable patient-care time, many physicians have been forced to limit practice scope from global availability, where the patient is located, to a silo of activity in the office or hospital. Travel time to see patients at different locations has become a luxury that is nonproductive and unbillable for patient care. Nonphysician extenders, such as nurse practitioners and physician assistants, have been increasingly employed to augment the number of daily patient visits and the number of sites for providing care but receive 85 percent of the usual payment allowed by Medicare and many health insurance companies unless the extender is directly supervised by a physician. These attempts to maintain or boost revenue for the small business medical practice result in decreased patient and physician face-to-face time either by limiting locations for access or by substituting other health-care providers instead of the doctor.

Another current health-care economic burden includes the lingering cost of medical education, which affects physician behavior that, in turn, can affect health-care costs. Income is a reward in a profession that consumes a doctor's time with working 50-55 hours a week as reported for 2007.[154] Physician income, however, is a delayed return on an educational investment which often consists of debt. New physicians have 10-15 years of training after high school while accumulating, as reported in 2012, an average debt of $162,000. Most new physicians begin practice between the ages of twenty-eight and thirty. The average obligation increased to $207,000 in 2015.[155] These educational loan repayment obligations begin when post-medical school training is completed unless the physician contracts for military or government service either during training or upon completion of training.[156] Part of the incentive for physicians preferring to become hospitalists or government employees with guaranteed salary rather than establishing an outpatient practice with uncertain income can be ascribed to the debt accumulated during lengthy and expensive medical education.

Physician behavior is also influenced by the evolving economic types of physician employment. The developing economic structures that determine a physician's workspace can be distilled into three basic formats that have profound effects on behavior in the physician-patient relationship. First, as an increasing employment type, many physicians and physician extenders are employees of a hospital system or insurance company. That is, the hospital, insurance company, or large physician billing company determines the physician workspace. This situation is analogous to the slave/indentured physician of ancient Greece and Rome in that physician activities are controlled by the employer. For example, if the physician is employed only in the hospital, the duration of the doctor-patient relationship necessarily is short although some hospitals have developed outpatient physician offices, thereby allowing development of long-term doctor-patient relationships. The hospital-influenced medical decisions are motivated by a need to reduce, but not eliminate, patient days in the hospital as attempts occur to maximize hospital revenue influenced by achievement in meeting measures imposed by reviewing organizations and payers. Standardization of care is used to meet these goals through the use of protocols. Algorithms as the means of standardization become a major decision determinant for patient care, and adherence to the algorithm replaces the doctor-patient relationship as the definition of quality care.

A second business choice for physicians is to partner with a medical business in an accountable care organization (ACO) or other partnership as a joint venture. Depending on the intellectual capital and the personal energy invested by caregivers into such partnerships, medical treatment can be innovative and responsive to the needs of individual patients while overall care improves for specific patient populations. However, most of these partnerships' decisions heavily weigh in favor of the business aspects regarding patient care for the sake of remaining financially solvent. Physicians may be encouraged to start and remain as junior partners or limited partners in these organizations which, therefore, reduce personal financial risks for physicians. However, reducing physician financial stake in such organizations may reduce physician involvement in decisions about the expenditures for medical care. Physician participation in the organization may be to provide only routine medical care as incentives may align with expense reduction rather than health-care innovation.

A third business model that is growing in the United States is concierge medical care. This model may be a natural evolution of traditional private practice, both solo and group, in response to payer intrusion into the doctor-patient relationship. The business model allows the maximum development of a doctor-patient relationship as physician expenses do not dictate the rendering of medical care. Office-based care costs are controlled by eliminating much of the billing expense. Payment occurs upfront with a set subscription fee. This payment system reduces practice overhead removing the need for many billing personnel. However, the concierge physicians tend to stay in the outpatient office and may remain uninvolved in direct care when the patient is hospitalized. Referrals are used to temporarily transfer care not covered by the subscription. Care by the referral physician is usually paid by standard health insurance. Concierge physicians also necessarily limit the number of patients enrolled in a physician panel to about 500, allowing more time with the patient.[157] For the 2019 United States population, about 662,000 primary care physicians would be needed for concierge medical services covering everyone. In 2016, only 953,695 physicians were licensed in the United States in all areas of practice and research.[158] In 2019, 479,856 physicians practiced primary care, which is needed for concierge coverage for the entire United States.[159] These facts mean the number of participating primary care physicians is insufficient to provide coverage for the whole United States population. Thus, this concierge model for improved patient care and relationship has limited application mainly because of a lack of enough primary care providers.

Influences outside of medical bill payments and outside of the doctor-patient relationship have also changed provider behavior. Changes in provider behaviors are illustrated by two developments over recent years. First, guideline/algorithm/protocol use has become commonplace in physician offices, outpatient care units, and inpatient care units. Guidelines are attempts to improve patient outcomes by providing a standard therapeutic approach to various diseases. Such tools have been embraced by payers, reviewers, and litigators as establishing standard and usual care. However, algorithms, for example, seem to follow the Pareto 80/20 Principle that is used in business analysis in that 80 percent of the patients are effectively treated by the algorithm decision points.[160] The other 20 percent of patients are likely to have too complex an illness or an illness that is not addressed by the algorithm. Vilfredo Pareto, a nineteenth-century Italian economist, described a split between effects and causes by noting that 80 percent of sales was made by 20 percent of the salesmen. However, the 80/20 split seems to occur in other areas of activity as noted by Dhand, et al., in the hospital setting, including 80 percent of nursing calls are from 20 percent of the patients. The enhancement of physician decision-making provided by algorithms follows the Pareto Principle by improving decision-making for 80 percent of the physicians while adding little to the quality of medical care provided by highly skilled physicians and other highly competent caregivers.[161] Important to remember is that algorithms tend to bring the quality of medical decisions and medical care to a mean level rather than raise that level to universal excellence. Whichever direction guidelines and algorithms push medical care, the medical decisions are not made within the doctor-patient relationship.

The second development in behavior occurs because of using truncated medical information known as the electronic health record. These software programs require voluminous data entry by medical professionals, who may have minimal computer and keyboard skills. To reduce the need for keyboarding, templates are frequently used with standard entries for the medical record. "Cut-and-paste" database function allows repetition of entries in medical records over multiple dates. Although discouraged, texting style jargon sometimes enters the medical record. Inability to spell or type leads to nonsense words in the permanent record since spell-check programs are not automatically provided. Using the draft or incomplete status for a hospital medical record leads to a stream-of-consciousness-like charting of the patient's hospital course without completing thoughts about the changes in disease status. Comprehensive generic statements tend to be inserted into the medical record text while specific information and discourse on the patient's disease process may not be stated. Hence, the medical information in active medical records tends to be generic and less meaningful for an individual patient's care. The patient's record becomes generic rather than being contextualized by the doctor-patient relationship for what is important to the patient.

What can be lost in the current stampede to electronic health care is the importance of the doctor-patient relationship for medical care decisions. Technological and business aspects of medical practice have become drivers of decisions about medical care. Doctors have been immersed in a technological world for which they generally have no training.[162] Confusion about medical care goals is increased by laws and regulations affecting medical practice, small businesses, and payment systems that are oriented towards population outcomes rather than towards individualized care for patients. Disrupting individualization of medical care and imposing business stresses on health-care providers combines with the rising costs for medical care to bring a conclusion that the current way of delivering medical care in America is not sustainable.

— FIVE —

The Way We Should Go

I f we accept the concept that quality health care, which leads to better patient outcomes and high patient satisfaction, is focused by the doctor-patient relationship, applying that concept to the American health-care system raises important questions. Can the rising cost of medical care be contained and made affordable for anyone in the society who desires health care? Can the quality of health care provided for a patient be continuously improved and occasionally innovated? I think the answer is "Yes," but actualizing that answer will require a cataclysmic health-care sector change that is neither simple nor readily accomplished.

First, it must be recognized that health care has changed from generally acute disease and injury management to mostly chronic disease management. Secondly, payment systems must be based on total patient management over time, such as a year or perhaps longer, rather than single point-of-service billable events. The control of expenditures for total patient management must go through the hands of the medical professional manager of the health care with advice and consent of the patient. Thirdly, the patient medical record must be completely portable. Fourthly, the Uber-generation mentality needs to be applied to health-care procurements to increase competitive pricing and availability. Fifthly, physician and provider attitudes and practices must be changed from a silo or shift-based mentality to a flexible team care approach led by the expert in the patient's current disease state. Whoever is the expert on the patient's primary chronic problem will change as the patient's disease state changes. Sixthly, the patient must have a stake in the health-care process regarding both the cost and the reward. Seventhly, payers, especially government payers, must not continue to use the ability to micromanage medical treatment and costs as resulting rules and regulations limiting prescribed care also limit innovation. Eighthly, medical care facilities and institutions must become more flexible in purpose and activity. Ninthly, the development, production, and distribution of cost-effective medications and therapies needs to be affordable for the patient while providing enough revenue to fund costly pharmaceutical research. Partial implementation of these nine changes may temporarily help control medical costs or quality issues. However, incomplete refocusing of the medical industry onto chronic care through the lens of the doctor-patient relationship will not alter the movement towards insolvency for the American health-care system.

To reform American health care, the target of these nine areas of change is the point-of-service for the patient as handled within the doctor-patient relationship. Global policies, regulations, and payment systems need to be modified to support individualized health care. Emphasis on individuals involved in health care, the doctor, the patient, and sometimes the family, necessitates restriction on micromanagement of that individualized health care by business and government. Limiting micromanagement by non-providers reduces or ends intercalation of payers and regulators between the physician and the patient when medical service is given. Failure to end micromanagement with insertion of various entities between doctor and patient will ultimately lead to a collapse of the personalized health care system we prize in America.

First – Acute to Chronic Care

Only in the last century has acute and subacute disease been transformed into chronic disease. An example is the effects from the discovery of insulin on the life expectancy of diabetic patients.[163] Diabetic patients no longer commonly die of untreated hyperglycemia. Instead, the duration of the disease and the treatment of the disease have transformed diabetic care into chronic disease management. Diabetic patients are, as a group, the population most likely to have renal failure, amputations, and adult-onset blindness.[164] These complications of diabetes are not necessarily life-ending but are manifestations of malady states that can persist many years.

Another example of disease transformation is found with heart ailments, especially coronary artery disease treatment, which has changed from passive therapy of bedrest as given to Lyndon Johnson to active therapy of revascularization, which has lowered the death rate by more than half from 1980 to 2000.[165] While controversy remains regarding use of the operating room versus the catheterization lab for the best results in ischemic heart disease therapy, death rates for the disease have fallen. Indeed, mortality from ischemic heart disease dropped from about 90 per 100,000 in 2005 to about 60 per 100,000 in 2015.[166] Longevity with heart disease has increased converting ischemia heart disease from an acute to a chronic condition.

A third example of disease transformation is the conversion of acute and sub-acute renal failure to chronic kidney disease with the use of dialysis and kidney transplantation, especially after funding for therapy in 1972. At the time the law was passed to fund dialysis, 25,000 patients were considered eligible for treatment out of 55,000 Americans with known kidney disease.[167] Now, instead of dying within weeks or months as was common at that time, some people continue to receive care as transplant or dialysis patients for over thirty years. In 2016, more than 610,000 people lived with renal failure replacement therapy.[168]

Consequent to the transformation of acute and sub-acute diseases into chronic diseases is an increased use of resources. An example of increased resource utilization is the number of doctor visits. Fee-for-service visits in the distant past consisted of office visits for specific wellness issues such as pregnancy, new baby exams, and immunizations, or acute illness and injuries. In 1991, 73 percent of patients had four or fewer doctor visits in a year.[169] In 2015, the per capita annual doctor office visit rate was four,[170] illustrating that most people did not see a doctor every year. However, development of a chronic disease changed those metrics for several groups of patients. For example, diabetic patients acquire a group of providers, including the primary care physician, endocrinologist, cardiologist, podiatrist, ophthalmologist, retinal specialist, and nephrologist, who will each see the patient three or more times a year. Hospitalizations and procedures for a diabetic patient add to the number of fee-for-service encounters each year. Another population, heart failure patients, have an average of twenty-three doctor visits per year.[171] Procedures with high fees are frequently used for these cardiac disease patients. The increased number of health care interactions is, perhaps, best illustrated by the chronic kidney failure patient. A typical in-center hemodialysis patient will have more than 150 fee-for-service health-care encounters, including dialysis treatments, per year. While the nephrologist is paid a monthly fee for dialysis united services, the fee is based on the number of patient visits in the month. Bundling of payments to the dialysis clinic for dialysis treatments is still based on per-session care, which is basically a fee-for-service payment. Fee-for-service visits with a primary care physician, surgeons, medical sub-specialists, and hospitals add to the number of billings per year for the dialysis patient. As found for other patients with chronic disease, payments covering dialysis-related and non-dialysis-related care for the dialysis patient remain fee-for-service based on the acute care model that has persisted in American medicine.

Therefore, acknowledging the expense that chronic disease management generates when using an acute care fee-for-service model is the first step to controlling costs. Increasing the dialysis population by 50 percent over the next five years, for example, would increase billable encounters by 30 million per year, if the number of encounters per patient per year remains stagnant. The president's executive order aims to reduce the increase in dialysis patients over ten years but does not have specific mechanisms to accomplish the plan.[172] However, successful dialysis means success in prolonging a life affected by several co-morbidities, which worsen as those diseases follow their usual course. Thus, chronic kidney disease management will necessarily involve long-term control of several complex, co-existing diseases that produce significant morbidity in the dialysis patient.

Successful change from an acute-care management approach to a chronic-disease management approach requires a team mentality, as no one person can orchestrate all aspects of the total care. Paying for team care requires a change in payment structure from a single event payment to global care payment over the specified time covered by the payment. Furthermore, flexibility in attitudes of providers is needed when more than one chronic disease is present necessitating the use of multiple caregivers. Patient care and money allocation for that care should be controlled by the disease expert for the current most active disease process until a different disease process becomes the primary problem. Thus, the role of team leader may be filled by different people determined by the patient's medical condition. Decisions about money allocation and care decisions must be filtered by the doctor-patient relationship with the patient having input about resource allocation including money. Finding solutions for the health-care financial crisis depends on understanding that management of care has changed from treating acute or temporary conditions to treating multiple chronic conditions in longer lived people. Furthermore, successful management of chronic diseases depends on involving the patient for resource allocation.

Second - Payment System

Health-care payment systems continue to be fee-for-service with total costs increasing as the number of services increases. As the patient population grows older and greater in number of older persons, medical expense necessarily increases individually and nationally. Attempts to control costs include imposition of threshold requirements for payment eligibility and fines, known as payment withholds or recoupment, for providers designated as poorly performing by not meeting payer-determined medical and regulatory goals. Government and corporate payers have imposed a variety of thresholds, including electronic medical record requirements, meaningful use tests, pay-for-performance measurement goals, authorization processes, and chart audit outcomes. All these threshold regulations increase the compliance-related overhead costs for providers while maintaining a fee-for-service acute-care mentality for payments. The physician is forced to hire employees, who do not generate revenue, for dealing with claims and compliance issues. Through regulations constraining medical decisions and forcing increased overhead, cost control measures by payers lead to the insertion of the payer between the physician and the patient.

Another attempt to control costs is through shifting payment responsibility to the patient by mandated deductible costs and co-payment costs. As these costs apply to different aspects of medical service, there are increasing patient complaints about unaffordable medications and health-care visits. Furthermore, there is little incentive for patient compliance in this system as deductibles and co-pays are viewed more as penalties than reasons to be proactive and interactive with the care. Some patients respond to the out-of-pocket expenses by declining to obtain nonemergency medical services. Increasing regulations, increasing physician overhead to comply with regulation and patient nonparticipation in pursuing cost-effective health care adversely impact the national health-care bill. Without a change in the payment system, health-care economics will collapse under the weight of increasing regulation, physician overhead, and patient nonparticipation.

Thus, an attempted bridge system between fee-for-service and comprehensive care payment systems was instituted in 1983 by the Medicare program for hospitals in the form of diagnosis-related group (DRG) payments.[173] However, the DRG payment system is an intensity-driven revenue system for a hospitalization, treating each hospitalization as a fee-for-service event and not a global payment for patient care over time in or out of the hospital. That is, the hospital lump sum payment is based on the number and severity of diagnoses listed during the hospitalization. For physicians, global payments have been tried for surgeon fees. These payments are like the DRG payment system in that the surgical procedure payment covers the care provided before and after that procedure. The Medicare policy for global surgical fees is expected to be changed because fewer physician visits were made than expected.[174] Both payment systems mistake a hospitalized episode of patient care as equivalent to chronic disease management.

As another attempt to address health-care costs, health maintenance organizations (HMO) and government demonstration projects using both accountable care organizations and pay-for-performance models have been tried with variable success. The HMO model started as a subscription service to build rural hospitals but grew into a means to reduce health-care cost increases through restricting hospitalizations and obtaining physician services at a discounted price.[175] Instead of developing into a prepaid health-care management system for chronic disease management and for health maintenance, the HMO system became focused on restricting costs for individual services, thereby leading to the passage of more than 900 state laws governing HMO practices.[176] The pay-for-performance demonstration project showed mixed benefits but was based on fee-for-service payments adjusted by penalties or bonuses, as described by Lyle Nelson in 2012.[177] Interestingly, Nelson also reported that the coronary bypass surgery global payment, split between the hospital and physicians, resulted in an average 10 percent decrease in Medicare expenditures without any change in patient outcomes. This lesson regarding benefits and cost efficiency of a global payment system based on partnership between health care providers seems to be lost on designers of subsequent health-care projects. Notably for most HMOs and government demonstration projects, the physician is seen as an expense or a generator of expense while the patient is seen as a passive recipient of benefits. These attitudes reinforce the fee-for-service mentality about health care within HMOs and federal government demonstration projects.

As another option, global payment for a chronic disease management or the enhancement of good health can be made annually to providers per patient as a capitation. The capitation system is currently controlled by payers and intermediary companies but would need to be directed to doctors instead. This system can work if the annual dollar amount paid per person is stable over several years and is accessible to the patient in ways analogous to a health savings account (HSA). A stable payment amount can lead to better-informed health-care decisions by the patient based on a budget that realistically allocates resources. An annual lump sum per patient also allows the payer to budget total annual costs. Budgeting would also be done by the doctor, which allows not only forecasting income and expenditure by the health-care provider but also a framework for decisions about effective allocation of financial resources.[178] However, decisions about the expenditures need to be made within the framework of the doctor-patient relationship so that the treatments remain consistent with the patient's desires. The resulting determinations would reflect a patient's personal stake in the outcome as tempered by the knowledge and compassion of the health-care provider who also has a professional, emotional, personal, and financial stake in the outcome. More importantly, control of the "purse" through this doctor-patient relationship may avoid redundant tests and therapies as the care is more easily tailored to the needs and desires of the patient while eliminating redundancy. This focus of expenditures through the doctor-patient relationship will also help reduce cost by encouraging a shift in the site of service back to the office from the emergency room and to outpatient infusion and ambulatory surgical centers from inpatient acute care hospitals.

As a resource for capitation, analyzing claims data from the Medicare database can provide initial estimates of the annual average costs for most chronic diseases. The annual global payment rates can be updated as claims data is analyzed. However, just as in the use of actuarial data to determine various types of insurance premiums requires several years of life expectancy data, so the adjustments in global payments must be based on several years of disease-specific health data. Different from the rules of the Affordable Care Act that allow the Secretary of Health and Human Services to change annually the operating rules for the health insurance products, chronic disease treatment global payments amounts should be based on five years of data with adjustments applied at the end of a one-year review. Using five years of data would allow a more complete analysis of costs and benefits regarding any new health-care treatment process. The one-year review time would allow innovations to be implemented while allowing time for practices to adjust to changes in the budgeted capitation. However, this capitation system would involve capitated and fee-for-service health care.

How would this payment system work? Using End-Stage Renal Disease (ESRD) as an example can illustrate how a combination capitation and fee-for-service payment system can be formed. The

2011 annual cost for an in-center hemodialysis patient was $87,945 per Medicare analysis but was $125,871 per patient in the Truven Health Market Scan (THMS) dataset).[179] A capitated payment would be based on all reasonable datasets. As reasonable beginning, total care allotment for the ESRD patient would be $90,000 per year. The money would be collected for a group of patients covered by a nephrology practice. If that practice cared for 2,000 dialysis patients, the pool of money available would be $180,000,000. Because of holiday- and vacation-associated reduction of supporting resources at the end of the calendar year, use of a fiscal year for payment decisions may be needed. The debate for the payment plan would focus on how that money is distributed, who controls the purse strings, and how effective money use is determined.

As leader of the team, the nephrologist would be paid $500 a month for all care, both outpatient and inpatient. The nephrologist would prescribe and monitor dialysis-related care. Services by other physicians and medical entities would be coordinated with dialysis care. Quality evaluation of the nephrologist would be based on morbidity-adjusted summation measures including survival, patient quality of life assessment, and completeness of medical records which includes documentation of team leadership. Quality micro-measures currently used by the Center for Medicare and Medicaid Services (CMMS) for rating dialysis clinics, such as calcium levels, hemoglobin levels, erythropoietin use, foot checks, flu shots, and a multitude of other parameters, would need to be rolled into a composite score showing success in achieving a percentage of academic and nephrology society-set patient care goals. While achieving 75 percent of these goals may be a reasonable means to score physician activities, these scores need to be based on intent-to-treat interventions to improve health status rather than on an arbitrary number. Factors other than physician prescription influence an outcome including patient frailty, patient compliance, patient intercurrent disease, staff compliance with administration of a therapy, and availability of the therapy from the manufacturer. For example, if a patient has recurrent abruptly developing problems with severe anemia after erythropoietin-like drugs are stopped, the quality goal would be to avoid the severe anemia rather than avoidance of that drug use. This goal is different from one of the past CMMS goals mandated for dialysis clinics to stop using erythropoietin if the patient had a certain anemia status defined by a hemoglobin above 11 grams per 100 milliliters. Rather, the targeted number for each health-care goal should be contextualized by the patient's health status, desires about treatment, and history of response to the attempted treatment.

Patient satisfaction with achieving individualized care quality, satisfaction with the proposed goals, and the composite care measures should constitute quality measure goals. Failure to satisfy the quality measure goals for a group of clinic patients would lead to ineligibility for the team leader nephrologist to participate in profit sharing associated with the global patient payment for the subsequent year. However, participation in profit sharing would resume after one year unless the outcomes attributable to the nephrologist fail to improve reaching the failed goals. Failure to participate in profit sharing for three successive years would remove the nephrologist from eligibility for the capitated payment patient care system for three years. However, a failure to prove the applied goals are conducive to improved care and outcomes would remove that penalty from the practicing nephrologists until new validated goals are implemented.

The primary care physician (PCP) would receive a capitation payment of $100 a month to provide health maintenance services for the patient. These provided services would be consistent with guidelines from the American College of Physicians (ACP) and the American Academy of Family Practice (AAFP). Included in the services would be immunizations, cancer screening, and evaluation of minor problems to avoid emergency room visits. Failure to perform the exam and completely document in the patient's portable medical record a summary of findings would cost the PCP $250 of the capitation with the sum used to perform the annual screening and immunization provision by another physician. That money would return to the risk pool fund for each patient.

In addition, dialysis services would require a capitation agreement with the dialysis organization based on CMMS dialysis payment rates. Participating in the capitation would provide immediate benefit to the dialysis company by remitting the total CMMS allowed payment rather than paying 80 percent of the allowable, as currently done by CMMS. For example, the base rate for outpatient dialysis was $231.55 in 2017 per treatment or $36,121.80 per year for 156 treatments. The new payment would be based on 160 treatments a year consisting of three sessions per week plus four extra sessions, if needed, totaling $37,048. As CMMS pays 80 percent of the allowed price, paying the total amount would increase clinic revenue for most patients by $7,409.60 per year. The dialysis clinic would be responsible to provide whatever outpatient dialysis is needed during the year without limit. The arbitrary limit of three treatment sessions a week would no longer be in effect. Furthermore, the dialysis clinic would be charged $50 daily for each hospital service day (inpatient, observation, or outpatient) with that money returning to the risk pool fund for that patient to help defray extra medical costs. A list of services included in the dialysis cost per treatment would be determined by CMMS, as is currently done. The list of services considered as a dialysis treatment would be updated by CMMS along with an updated payment rate per treatment affecting the annual capitation rate. While extra treatments to control edema and pulmonary edema would be included in the annual rate, the cost of medications that are not usually used in a routine dialysis treatment and transfusions would come from the non-dialysis medication and risk pools of money. Dialysis clinics also would be required to maintain Medicare certification and state licensing while fulfilling all the quality measures and quality improvement programs required by third-party entities including the federal government. Notably, list of services by the dialysis clinic covered by the capitated, lump sum payment would not be the maximum legal menu being provided by the dialysis clinic. Additional value of the provided services would be at the discretion of the dialysis clinic without obligating an increase in payment rate. Therefore, providing protein supplements or paying for a taxi ride for dialysis would not be prohibited. Instead, the dialysis clinic would have freedom to enhance patient health in ways that reduced hospitalizations and reduced co-morbidity acuity.

Because such hemodialysis patients have complex medical problems with multiple co-morbidities, money for catastrophic insurance would be needed. As a matter for discussion, it is assumed that $100 a month would purchase a suitable catastrophic health insurance policy. Insurance companies willing to provide the catastrophic insurance policies could also act as plan administrator. If a nephrology practice had 2,000 patients for the full year, the catastrophic health insurance company would receive $2,400,000 in premiums per year. With 300,000 dialysis patients being covered, the premiums for catastrophic insurance would be $360,000,000 per year. The catastrophic insurance would be activated when 90 percent of the patient's total annual budget is depleted and used to cover inpatient expenses at the usual CMMS rate, which is based on the DRG payment system. The financial risk for a catastrophic illness would not be borne by the patient.

Hospital payments could be done as a capitated payment, although such negotiations through nephrology practices may prove too complex. However, based on a mean cost of $12,600 per hospitalization with an average of two hospitalizations for each dialysis patient per year,[180] $25,200 would be set aside for the hospital pool. Hospital payments would be based on the CMMS DRG payment menu. A hospitalization cost beyond $25,200 would be covered by the risk pool monies. It is expected that the catastrophic insurance would cover prolonged hospitalizations including rehabilitation. Again, CMMS would provide the policies and regulations about payments for hospital readmissions and hospital acquired diseases.

To ensure efficient use of payments for access maintenance, these procedures would be done in the outpatient setting. Vascular centers would need to be capitated at $10,000 per patient per year anticipating coverage of two procedures a year. Capitation would provide $3 billion a year for access centers to maintain 300,000 patients. Peritoneal dialysis catheter placement would also be covered by the capitation. The capitation monies would also cover physician fees. However, the access center would refund $2,000 to the risk pool fund when access failure required hospital-based services.

To support the outpatient treatment of hemodialysis patients, a pool of money is needed to cover medical costs outside of the usual dialysis treatment. If $200 per patient per month is set aside to pay for these therapies as an outpatient, 2,000 patients would generate a pool of $4,800,000, which should cover most medications and durable medical equipment unrelated to dialysis. Transfusions would be covered by this pool of money, as well. The administering insurance company would be encouraged to obtain pharmaceutical distributors at the best price for the patients.

Another pool of money would be needed to cover services by other providers including podiatrists, cardiologists, surgeons, endocrinologists, pulmonologist, gastroenterologists, wound care providers, and physical therapists. Fee-for-service payments based on Medicare rates could be covered with $3,800 a year for most patients based on a level-four office visit as defined by Medicare. In-office procedures would also be included in this pool.

Administration of the capitated policy would require the expertise and vendor relationships of health insurance companies or Medicare/Medicaid intermediaries. Responsibilities for the administrator would include tracking costs, reconciling accounts, collecting quality metrics, contracting vendor relationships with the advice and consent of the lead physician or lead medical practice, and distributing payments. However, determinations of covered care would not be done by the administrator of funds. Thus, personnel costs would be reduced for the intermediary company. Administration fee would be $100 per patient per month. Thus, for 300,000 dialysis patients, $30,000,000 would be paid to the administration companies. In return for optimizing health-care plan administration for the benefit of the patient and the patient's health-care desires, the administration company would participate in profit sharing.

The remaining $1,952 would be placed into an interest-bearing risk pool account to cover unexpected illness, expensive medications, and prolonged hospitalization. Indeed, a lump-sum payment should be initially delivered to an interest-bearing account with the interest benefitting the patient's medical care funding. The risk pool account could also be used to compensate patients for untoward outcomes from medical errors. Compiling the various pools of money may look like this:

Nephrologist care	$500/month	$6,000.00
PCP	$100/month	$1,200.00
Dialysis	160 treatments/year	$37,048.00
Catastrophic insurance	$100/month	$1,200.00
Hospital DRG	$12,600/admission	$25,200.00
Access center cap		$10,000.00
Non-dialysis related care	$200/month	$2,400.00
Point-of-service		$3,800.00
Risk pool		$1,952.00
Administration	$100/month	$1,200.00
Total		$90,000.00

By pooling payments for a cohort of dialysis patients within a nephrology practice providing dialysis, catastrophic expenses can be covered by a combination of catastrophic health insurance and the risk-pool fund. For example, 2,000 dialysis patients would have risk pool funds of $3,922,048. Allocation adjustments could be based on the individual market economics impacting the cost of doing business, but adjusting global payment by local rent prices, for example, should be limited to avoid stimulating local rent inflation. Increased need for a non-ESRD-related service could be met by capitation rather than fee-for-service. Prices for such services would be based on local negotiations between the management nephrologists and other physicians with payment from the non-dialysis-related care pool. Management by the nephrology practice needs to be robust and proactive, requiring a partnership of medical business and nephrology practice expertise. Because business goals and medical therapy goals are not always identical, the lead decision and budget formulation need to rest in the hands of the nephrologist, who is charged with protecting benefit for the patient first, then the nephrology practice, then the business interests. As a benefit from local management of funds, innovation in medical care could be unhindered by arbitrary rules, regulations, and pre-authorizations. Instead, monitoring innovative medical care would be done through peer-reviewed processes that could be funded from the risk-pool money. Thus, each nephrology practice could become a small experimental lab for producing the best care at the best price on a real-time basis. These principles could apply to all physician teams treating any chronic medical problem.

Moreover, incentives would arise from this method of handling residual monies from payments for patients upon successfully completing the fiscal year. About $33,352 of the allocated money reflects variable health-care expenses that may consume the pooled money. Successful management by the physician and effective participation by the patient may lead to a reduction in medical cost during the year. That is, physicians' and patients' co-management of costs would be encouraged for the fiscal decision process. Failure in almost all health cost-reduction schemes partly reflect a lack of inclusion of the patient as an active participant in the medical care process. Success and failure of a treatment plan hinge on patient compliance, but this simple fact is often ignored. Furthermore, if a treatment plan is formulated within the doctor-patient relationship and results in a "good" outcome, the patient should be rewarded. An easy reward would be to take 10 percent of the net profit from the annual fund to be deposited into a patient-owned HSA. Currently, a Medicare patient cannot contribute to the HSA, and this incentive plan would require a new law by Congress. However, a patient incentive plan should funnel the money into covering health-care costs. Distributing profit to the patient through the HSA would ensure the money is used for medical costs and allow the patient to build an account that could be inherited by the family to pay for future medical expenses. After the 10 percent is taken from the profit, the United States government would want a partial refund, which could be obtained as a tax. The remaining profit could be taxed at either the capital gains tax rate or a corporate tax rate for small businesses. Post-tax money would be given to the at-risk participants with 30 percent going to the lead physician, 20 percent going to the supporting physicians and/or health-care entity, and 20 percent going to the dialysis company. The remainder of the profit could be split evenly among all participants in the patient's health care. While the profit for excellent care would be small per individual patient, larger groups of patients might provide an opportunity for practice profit while providing incentive for the development of innovative, cost-effective care. Therefore, it is possible for all participants – patients, providers, and payers – to win.

The same format could be used for low morbidity patients as well. Primary care services could be capitated and prepaid for the year. As an example, a single person, not requiring chronic disease maintenance, would cost $5,400 per year while a couple would cost $7,200 per year, and a family with up to three children would cost $9,600 per year. Primary care services covered would include "wellness" check-ups, nonemergency medical problem visits, immunizations, and disease screening based on the current recommendations of the American College of Physicians and American Association of Family Practitioners. The primary physician would be paid $50 per person per month. The physicians would save overhead expenses including billing staff salaries, costs to appeal nonpayment, and costs to request prior authorizations. Insurance for catastrophic medical problems would be needed at $100 per person per month. Another $75 per person per month would fund an account, such as an HSA, to pay for medications and would be owned by the patient. Administration of the plan and arranging pharmacy benefits would be done by the insurance agency for $50 per person per month. Another $200 a month would be used for a contingency fund that would also provide money for hospitalization and referred medical services. Money from the contingency fund could accrue, allowing funding of single events such as genetic sequencing for prognostic and therapeutic purposes or for pregnancy care. This program could produce health insurance for a healthy person costing $450 a month. For a couple, money allotments would be changed by doubling payment for the primary physician, medical savings account, and the managing insurance agency. A family of five could be covered for $800 a month if the extra $200 is allotted to encourage family-group medical care. The primary physician would receive an extra $50 per month while the medication fund and the insurance agency would receive an extra $25 per month. The remaining $100 would increase catastrophic health insurance. Unused contingency funds would be awarded to participants in a manner like the chronic disease management plans. That is, 10 percent of the profit would fund a patient-owned HSA, and, after the government taxes paid for the remaining 90 percent of the profit, leftover money would be divided among the providers of care including the insurance company. A possible division of money would be 30 percent for the primary care physician, 30 percent for the insurance company, 30 percent among the participating providers not at financial risk, and the remainder divided among all participating providers, including the patient to the patient's HSA. This style of distribution of health-care dollars seeks to instill a universal awareness of medical costs while encouraging a team approach to improve efficiency and effectiveness of provided services. Moreover, the patient becomes a beneficiary of both the care and savings from financial efficiencies in that care.

Third – Personal Medical Record

Success in patient care is heavily influenced by timely access to accurate medical data. The electronic health record (EHR) has been mandated by federal law as a section of the American Recovery and Reinvestment Act of 2009, seeking to coerce the types of data recorded in hopes that medical decisions will be improved.[181] Unfortunately, the effect has been to focus attention on data acquisition through the electronic record rather than the portability of data throughout the patient's life. The only truly portable system remains the United States military system of physical charts hand-carried by the military or military-dependent patient. What caused the problem for civilians? Congress, through the HITECH Act of 2009, which is a section of the American Recovery and Reinvestment Act of 2009, mandated what was documented rather than how the data was documented. The law stimulated exuberant growth of the electronic health-care software industry resulting in many systems that, unfortunately, fail to communicate with each other. Occasionally, the demise of the EHR vendor or a decision to change the EHR vendor has threatened loss of patient-specific medical data because software databases recording medical information are considered proprietary. A portable health-care record conceptually requires that the various health-care medical record systems communicate what occurs at each point of service. However, recent Health and Human Services 2018 guidelines consider interoperability to be voluntary as explained in a recent guideline: "[I]nteroperability refers to the ability of two or more products, technologies, or systems to exchange information and to use the information that has been exchanged without special effort on the part of the user. EHR and EDC systems may be noninteroperable, interoperable, or fully integrated, depending on supportive technologies and standards."[182]

What was not recognized is that portability failure of medical information reflects the nonexistence of a common library defining the database terms. Each EHR software vendor has a proprietary definition for each medical term used to populate the database field in the record. To allow transfer of medical information, the medical term used in one EHR system must be translated into a corresponding definitive for the different EHR system. The costs to translate medical information from one provider, such as a laboratory service, allowing importation into another EHR, such as physician office records, are currently borne by the physician. As the patient interacts with multiple health-care entities using different EHR systems, multiple translations are needed to electronically update the primary patient record. Each translation creates a separate charge to the physician office. To avoid forcing increased provider costs for translating data from one electronic record to another, Congress should mandate that all health-care terms and definitions be standardized. This standardized dictionary should be used by all electronic health-record software companies before the software is certified for Medicare patients. Therefore, the Library of Congress, by federal law, should be charged with maintaining the list of terms and definitions. In database terms, the Library of Congress should define data fields, that is, the software vocabulary, and Congress should mandate Medicare certification be limited to health-care software vendors that use those definitions. Of note, Congress should neither mandate how the electronic health record operates nor the focus of that record system. The nature of the medical practice and software interaction with the providers and the patients should determine operating parameters and focus. However, use of a standard library of health-record terms would facilitate collection of data from all electronic health records for government use if certification stipulated software vendors must provide encrypted and de-identified patient data for government retrieval. Patients, medical care providers, and the United States government would benefit from the portability of medical data, which would also aid reducing duplicated services. Only the software vendors would lose revenue, but total costs to medical providers for EHR systems would be more easily controlled.

Expense for developing the definition library for database fields would be borne by the United States government, but the software companies would be responsible for bringing their database products into standardization for certification. Encryption technology would need to be added so that de-identified medical data could be transmitted to CMMS for analysis and subsequent policy decisions. Software companies already employ people to link different database products and may be able to comply quickly with the mandate to use a common library of terms. Cost savings to providers may be large by obviating the need to pay additional money for translation of a laboratory report or hospital record before inclusion into an office-based electronic record.

Moreover, the centralized collection of data imported into the portable patient electronic health record is essential to avoid duplication of services, leading to cost savings. More importantly, the composite record may reveal a hidden diagnosis or a subtle response to a therapy. Artificial intelligence algorithms can be used to help prevent duplicated services and augment health maintenance by generating alerts for the practitioner responsible for a patient's medical care. When genetic data, such as the "Mega Database," can also be incorporated into the routine health record, further benefits may accrue including prediction about future diseases and medication responses. Failure to have a completely portable patient health record is probably the most important impairment to changing medical treatment from being an isolated event into being a part of life-long health care.

Fourth – Supply and Customer Service

Lessons learned over the past three decades have shaped both supply and demand effects on business. For example, Toyota successfully used in-time supply of manufacturing parts to reduce the need for static storage spaces for car components.[183] Likewise, Uber developed a smart-phone-based transportation business that saved money and skirted many governmental business mandates and operating regulations. Additionally, Amazon developed a sales system that centralized storage and distribution of goods while increasing convenience for customers. All these companies survey customers about satisfaction regarding service for each interaction. Thus, a lesson for the health-care industry is that provision of excellent health care should satisfy the needs and desires of the patient while not being tied to brick and mortar or flexibility-reducing rules and regulations. As the Uber generation engages in health-care services, the demand will be for flexibly provided, excellent customer service with suitable follow-up and review.

This kind of customer service is an unspoken component of the successful doctor-patient relationship. Gaps in medical knowledge and misunderstandings about a diagnosis are viewed differently when the patient relationship with the doctor is personal versus impersonal. This difficulty stemming from an impersonal relationship occurs more commonly in the hospital. The hospital staff, seeing the patient for only a few days, has more difficulty than the long-term personal physician in establishing a personal relationship. The in-hospital problem with establishing a personal relationship develops because hospital work occurs in shifts while involving increased morbidity of the patient. Hospital staff also are required to spend increasing amounts of time documenting the patient's day, which keeps the staff sitting before a computer screen. Availability of hospital staff to interact with the patient tends to be reduced as business models are used to increase staff productivity. Productivity goals have become major determinants for staffing ratios and work assignments in many hospitals. Some hospitals have addressed patient dissatisfaction by reducing patient-to-nurse ratios or supplying a resource nurse, thereby allowing more flexibility for caregivers providing team-based care. However, a general shift in professional mindset to documentation has forced increased computer use as compared to what was present a century ago when compassion and interested care were the major focus of the hospital-based medical armamentaria.

Although restoring flexibility in the provision of care has begun, such flexibility faces resistance in institutionalized brick-and-mortar care sites. An example of new flexibility development is how outpatient procedures and home care are becoming feasible, reflecting technologic advancements and changes in patient comfort level. However, hospitals, nursing homes, rehabilitation centers, and surgical centers have brick-and-mortar related costs. Tied to these structural costs are costs for personnel to staff the buildings over twenty-four hours in many instances. An additional factor, federal payment rules were formed to cover these expenses including allowed per-item billing rates for emergency room services, location modifiers increasing payment for hospital-based outpatient services, and block payments for unfunded patients. Other payment rules have led to the inability to perform profitable out-of-hospital services, including transfusions, cardiac imaging procedures, and some infusions so that the patient must be returned to the hospital-based setting for financial considerations. Some payers participating in the health exchanges do not allow any outpatient procedures, thereby forcing admission for minor surgery.[184] Flexibility in allowing patient care in the outpatient, that is, out-of-hospital setting when such care can be done safely and comfortably would result in cost savings and better utilization of resources. The patient satisfaction with such care would increase when care can be done away from the hospital.[185]

Besides flexibility, follow-up in the Uber generation sense is more than a satisfaction survey. Follow-up implies an ability to continue or reengage services and provision of supplies in a timely manner. Just as the Toyota manufacturing plant is shut down by failure of in-time supply, patient care is interrupted by not providing needed medication, delaying needed testing, or limiting physical therapy. For example, failure to provide affordable insulin refills for a diabetic is likely to lead to an expensive hospitalization. As reported by National Public Radio in 2018, inability to afford the cost of insulin led a person to reduce or forego the medication, leading to premature death.[186] Another failure is found with withdrawal of financial coverage for ongoing physical therapy or exercise for an elderly patient recovering from a hip fracture who does not meet official criteria for improvement. The practical purpose of therapy and exercise is reducing increased risk for another fall and fracture rather than meeting an arbitrary improvement measure. Hence, completion of a course of therapy should be followed with maintenance care for that medical condition analogous to an Uber ride to a destination implying the need for an Uber ride home. Engaging medical care requires initiation, completion of initial therapy, and maintenance with adjustments based on the patient's medical and physical need. What is not useful for long-term health care is a preset term of engagement or arbitrary cessation of funding based on anything other than completion of that care. However, completion of medical care requires setting and following realistic goals for the outcome as well as formulating contingency plans for failure to succeed with the therapy. Setting and following realistic goals is best done through the doctor-patient relationship rather than through outside rule makers.

Additionally, using technology to match patient needs for competitively priced medical products is the greatest Uber lesson. Medication refills can be priced for online and neighborhood pharmacies. Therapy and exercise programs can be matched to the patient's needs as full-service inpatient programs, exercise classes at local gyms, or home-based therapy selected using comparative pricing and satisfaction ratings. Durable medical equipment and supplies would also figure into the health cost coverage equation. Competition improves pricing as found with Amazon selling medical supplies 10-20 percent below prices from usual vendors. Individualized patient care would be enhanced by matching therapeutic options with the patient's situation. When mobility is provided by the vendor to the patient's location, price and availability determine the purchasing pattern for medical supplies. Currently some states limit availability of services or locations through a certificate of need (CON) restriction. The CON is essentially a zoning process that seeks comments from both favorable and unfavorable parties about the necessity of the medical location or service before allowing issuance of the new license. Competition needs to be encouraged by changing laws and regulations that restrict sites of medical service or development of medical service through demanding a certificate of need. Thus, competition for business becomes the major factor for cost savings and provision of quality products and services.

Fifth – Solo to a Team

Changing health-care provider prescribing patterns, team-care perspectives, and flexibility in leadership attitudes is a challenge. Changing private practitioner prescribing patterns of medical care is most easily done by tying the education process to financial gain when the desired pattern is followed as shown in a 2016 Scotland study.[187] However, the Scottish physicians were isolated practitioners despite being employed by the national health-care service providing the education. American physicians often practice outside of training programs and government employment without federal control over nonnarcotic prescriptions. As prescription authority is controlled by the states in the United States, states are trying to influence prescribing patterns for controlled substances through electronic monitoring. Texas, for example, has mandated an online physician registry for prescribing controlled drugs. Eligibility to use that online site forces education completion.[188] Forced reeducation and compliance with third-party prescription regulations is thought, by many American practitioners, to be an overreach by payers and regulators leading to increased overhead costs and decreased physician efficiency.

Developing a team care perspective is impeded by financial and business pressures that reduce effective patient care time. In an attempted return to full-time direct patient care, many practice owner physicians have left solo and small-group practice for employment with only 47.1 percent of practices owned by physicians in 2016.[189] While technological and business matters are removed from the daily concern of the employed physician, productivity goals tend to be imposed by business practices, which can force physicians to engage in more but shorter fee-for-service encounters. As contrasted with self-employed physicians, the employed physicians' perspective may be conflicted since employer goals may differ from team-formulated, patient-centered objectives derived from a long-term relationship with the patient.

Physicians joining a physician-controlled group may still be paid on a fee-for-service-based system that, again, may develop a conflict between a business need and a patient-centric perspective. However, a few private practices are embracing full-risk payment models that include incentive payments for desired outcomes.[190] Medical care payment in this model does not reflect the number of fee-for-service encounters, thus fostering development of a long-term treatment plan with the patient by paying for long-term care. Team medical care can be developed as participants share revenue instead of competing for a restricted stream of revenue. This approach promotes care based on the doctor-patient relationship but has limitations based on availability of participating physicians and participating patients joining a capitation plan.

However, the ACO or capitation model may provide a means to change caregiver attitudes about team care if physicians assume corporate responsibilities in governance. By federal definition, ACO governance is by a partnership between business entities and physicians. For ACO effectiveness, physicians need to participate in the amalgamation of medical care objectives with business objectives. Such amalgamation requires knowledge about how quality care is provided, how patient participation in care is increased, how care teams are built, and how resources are efficiently utilized. Business training is needed for physicians who are involved in these activities, although obtaining a Master of Business Administration (MBA) with a medical business focus is not essential. Business training like the renal business weekend training program developed by the Renal Physicians Association and Duke University Fuqua School of Business can improve business skills. With business training, physician leadership can be effective for actualizing the premise of the team building led by the expert regarding the patient's primary disease. If the patient is included in the decision process, the business-trained medical care team can effectively control the expenditure of resources and money.

However, failure to emphasize the doctor-patient relationship and physician expert in controlling the provision of care may allow reversion to business-principle control of medical decisions based on budgets and profit. That is, compassionate, personalized care may be relegated to secondary importance in expenditure decisions regardless of team-care reasons. The lack of physician compassion in the medical business decisions can result in a Wells-Fargo-type scandal for medical care. That is, pressure to "sell" medical care can "lead to battered employee morale and [lead] to ethical breaches" as seen in the 2013 Wells Fargo occurrence.[191] Business success in medical practice needs to be analyzed as a process rather than the goal if patient care is truly the focus of the health-care industry. Team-based care can focus on the patient, especially if the patient is part of that team.

Changing attitudes about leadership flexibility and sharing the leader mantle involves modifying long-held perspectives. As has been seen in other aspects of American society, long-term changes in health-care provider perspectives and attitudes will necessitate changes in the training process. Currently, as medical school departments and divisions compete for money and prestige, including political power, medical training is impacted. Teaching sessions tend to stay within the departmental division for a limited audience with occasional "grand rounds" for everyone. Patient-care rounds tend to be made with a group from one service then separately by a group from another service until all the health-care services have taken different small groups of trainees to see the patient. Communication between the groups tends to be written chart notes read by few people. Thus, the training experience tends to reinforce a silo mentality for providing care.

The silo mentality is especially found in performing procedures, which in the 1970s was viewed as a team-member responsibility. Procedure training now tends to be limited to a few persons as if seeing but not performing a procedure during a medical school or residency-training rotation suffices for understanding indications, processes, and risks of that procedure. The consequence of this style of procedure training is the production of many health-care providers who have difficulty doing procedures while assuming that ordering a procedure is equal to having a procedure done well. Team responsibility for successful procedures is not present.

Another factor promoting silo mentality over team care during the past fifteen years has been changes limiting physician daily training time and workload. These rules essentially convert in-hospital residency training to shiftwork.[192] Shift training, which limits the time a resident physician can work, may limit learning and curtail medical skill acquisition.[193] More importantly, a silo mentality can become more easily ingrained by thinking that responsibility for care is limited to specific issues or time periods rather than the whole health of the patient.

Therefore, revamping training to emphasize individualized patient care may contribute to improving outcomes, patient satisfaction, and medical costs by developing team thinking and management. Acknowledging that internal quality improvement processes concerning morbidity, mortality, outcomes, patient satisfaction, and cost efficiency may require working with small groups and, sometimes, individual private settings. Multispecialty medical team training remains needed to universalize trainee perspectives through exposure to multiple approaches in medical care. Daily to weekly conferences for all trainees should be rotated among all departments and divisions of the training program fostering an eclectic approach to medical care. These conferences should be recorded and archived for easy retrieval by trainees. Multidisciplinary conferences using panel discussants formulating a care plan should be routine. An example would be a conference on the care for a patient with metastatic renal cell carcinoma. The patient's case would be presented to a urologist, oncologist, nephrologist, pharmacist, physical therapist, renal nurse, and other caregivers who may be involved in that patient's care. While medical care by committee must be avoided, the care plan discussion by a team of caregivers would provide valuable education.

In a teaching hospital setting, patients with complex diseases would benefit from care by a multidisciplinary team. Daily team rounds would consist of physicians representing multiple specialties and disciplines. Such a team could be the primary care or hospitalist team as the leader plus a cardiologist, pulmonologist, nephrologist, hematologist, and surgeon along with pharmacist and physical therapist rounding on fifteen to twenty patients. Not everyone on the team would contribute to the care of every patient. However, many hospitalized patients have complicated illnesses for which the care plan would benefit from contributions reflecting various perspectives. Hopefully, with team rounding, the physician trainee perspective changes from being on a service to taking care of a patient. More importantly, this form of physician training emphasizes communicating with team members and jointly formulating treatment plans. Therefore, the silo mentality of practice abates, and the concept of team care for patients is enhanced.

Sixth – Patient Involvement

One lesson learned from beneficiaries having completely free medical care without beneficiary obligation, such as occurs with Medicaid, is that medical care tends to be misused, becoming more expensive. Patient behavior has been estimated to affect 69 percent of total medical costs including $100,000,000,000 in additional cost because of poor compliance in taking medications.[194] Arguments to increase patient "skin in the game" tend to invoke up-front deducible and co-payment health-care costs. While such up-front patient-borne costs can be scalable to income status, the intent is encouraging the patient to seek comparative pricing for a service as a means to lower patient costs for health maintenance and wellness activities.[195] However, when direct patient payment is increased, an unintended consequence is that patients who purchase high-deductible health insurance plans tend to forego or delay medical care rather than select more cost-effective immediate medical care.[196]

Difficulty in determining how to effectively increase patient participation and responsibility to spend health-care dollars arises from misunderstanding what "patient skin in the game" means.

Studies and regulations have been formulated from the viewpoint of the economist, health-care payer, and government regulator. These entities, external to the patient-care provision, enact payment policies ostensibly for the good of the beneficiary. However, patient viewpoints are different as they have their actual skin, as well as other organs, affected by care and cost for care while retaining the need to pay ongoing day-to-day living expenses. Therefore, patient choice may be between paying for health care or rent. Balancing health-care spending with necessary (rent, food, electricity, transportation) and desired (cellphones, cable service, beer, fast food) expenses on a limited income will lead to personal preference directing spending choices. Such choices may be judged by health-care payers and providers to be unsophisticated, unwise, or excellent sacrifices of personal desires. However, third-party judging of spending choices may have no influence on the decisions by patients and families about these choices. Aligning patient health-care decisions with patient decisions about spending requires promoting personal health as a patient priority. Increasing patient skin in the game, that is, the patient establishing priority of personal health, occurs by increasing patient involvement in the health-care process by at least four concurrent mechanisms.

The first means of increasing patient involvement in health care is a return to conversation within the doctor-patient relationship. A monologue with a patient tends to leave the patient anxious about the disease process, confused about medical options, and uninspired to comply with prescriptive therapies. Conversation brings some parity to the relationship although the patient's education, intellect, severity of illness, and anxiety affect what the patient hears and understands. Attempts to explain an illness with possible therapeutic options can develop trust between physician and patient. These conversations foster increased understanding and openness to listening for the patient. Evidence about conversations with patients, from the 1970s and 1980s, has shown "that the most frequently used techniques, such as public and patient instruction, are not those shown to be the most effective in well-designed controlled trials."[197] In that 1982 study, Haynes advocated a combination of interventions, including (1) feedback to the patient, (2) patient rewards, (3) tailoring medication schedules for convenience, (4) encouraging family support, (5) engendering self-help, (6) negotiating behavior contracts, and (7) calling patients for office visit compliance. Time constraints limit the use of the entire health-care team for participation in conversation and education with the patient, but the leader or principal physician for that team must establish a conversational relationship with the patient that also allows other participants to enter the dialogue. Health-care providers also must be equipped through education in speech and debate techniques, psychology of conversation interactions, and group discussion techniques, allowing more effective participation in this interaction with patients. In addition, patients need to be prepared for participation in the health-care dialogue. Public education can be enhanced via schools, public broadcasting, churches, health forums, mail, and Internet materials. These educational activities need to equip patients for assuming an active role in the health-care process. Increasing medical conversation should be viewed as an active process requiring preparation by both the physician and the patient.

A second means of increasing patient involvement in health care and likely improving quality of outcomes is providing to the patient transparent analysis of true rather than billed costs of therapies. The true cost analysis must be contextualized by assessing likely benefits and risks of the therapies. Part of the analysis is presenting non-monetarized expense of medical care. Cost for a therapy includes time requirements, inconvenience from schedules, endurance of pain and suffering, desired and undesired responses to various medications, and use of resources for patient and family support. Comparison can then be made between the usual cash costs of different medical options using estimates from actuarial data. Intangible costs can be added to the analysis, leading to the most acceptable course of treatment for the patient. Important for this discussion is avoidance of microanalysis for every potential good or ill outcome for a therapeutic course such as outlined in FDA-mandated drug information inserts. Instead, medical information should be translated, by or for the physician, into layman's terms explaining the likely outcome for a disease and likely effects of a proposed therapy. Provision of this information can contribute to a clear and rational decision about therapy for an acute or chronic disease. As an additional benefit, this communiqué reduces the risk for later litigation.[198] Of course, such information must be clarified for the patient by the compassionate and concerned physician leading the health-care team. This information clarification requires a knowledge of the patient's health status, emotional status, and desires for the future. Medical record documentation of decisions should be done by documenting the preferred management process with anticipated costs. With this cost-benefit analysis, the patient and physician, with the health-care team, can decide which probable risks and likely consequences are worth the estimated costs.

A third means to motivate patient participation for optimal health care processes is providing a reward reflecting patient engagement in the process. The reward process must acknowledge decisions to accept or reject therapeutic options. That is, the reward cannot be contingent on accepting an edict from the prescribers or the payers. Such a reward would necessarily be a delayed gratification because linkage reflects the consequences of many decisions and actions. However, despite delayed gratification or payment, rewards can be an incentive for health-enhancing behavior. The carrot-and-stick model has mostly been used to change physician and corporate behavior. However, only the stick part of the model has been used for patients through deductible costs, co-payment charges, limitations in services, and limitations of therapeutic choices, especially pharmaceuticals. Attempts to change the patient into an engaged consumer and partner in health care are being tried without a monetary reward through providing home monitoring and immediate health feedback.[199] However, such limited patient reward platforms can serve the payees more than the patients.

Building a patient-centric reward system starts with recognition that using only one type of reward is insufficient to motivate all patients to engage in compliant and healthy behavior. A combination of emotional, preferential, and financially centered rewards is needed. Awards can be issued by medical and patient organizations tasked with establishing criteria encouraging patient engagement in the health-care system.

Emotional rewards include achieving better health and body image through following the appropriate regimen. Another emotional reward can be reduction in stress and anxiety when dealing with the health-care procurement process, especially if costs for services becomes transparent. Emotional rewards may also occur with periodic health report cards charting the successes and failures in improving health status. These rewards can be tailored to the patient's context, culture, and socio-economic status, encouraging patient joy with health care.

Preferential-based rewards could include social interactions with other patients and health-care workers through support groups, free admission to health-care seminars, or empowerment as a patient representative or leader advocating for the person's disease group. Preferential rewards could also be given as prizes for achievements in improving health status. Such awards could include a personal service for the patient, a shopping spree, or a paid vacation with other patients. However, preferential rewards should promote health care and not be cash.

Financial rewards for achieving cost-effective, high-quality outcomes need to be tied to the health-care system, reflecting performance by the health-care team, including the patient and patient's family. Cost savings for the payment plan should lead to profit sharing between providers and the patient. Because plan profit depends on participation by the patient to achieve effective and efficient total care over time, the patient contribution to a positive financial status from successful health management must be rewarded. Profit sharing needs to proportionally benefit the patient via a contribution to the patient-owned HSA. Otherwise, the patient only assumes the physical risk of a poor outcome from unsuccessful medical care. The multiplicity of rewards, emotional, preferential, and financial, are likely to interest many different personality types of patients, encouraging increased participation in improved, individualized health care.

A fourth means to increase patient involvement in health care arises from generating a knowledgeable health-care consumer. Measuring the average American medical knowledge has not been systematically done. Indeed, professional literature presented by Health Affairs in 2013 centered on definitions and structures for understanding patient knowledge under the framework of patient engagement rather than national measurement of American health knowledge.[200] However, a 2007 Swiss study revealed that most Swiss citizens knew less than 33 percent of minimal medical knowledge that was tested.[201] Needed is a national education effort to prepare Americans to be engaged patients. Systematic education should teach skills required to make medical decisions, to understand insurance payments for related decisions, and to create budgets dealing with medical expenses in the context of living expenses. Some remedial educational efforts may also be needed to teach basic math and reading skills to enable handling bank accounts and HSA accounts. As educational needs are not uniform, this initiative must rely on grassroots-level development and planning to address neighborhood and peer group needs. The emphasis should not be on anatomy or sex education, as may be found in public high schools, but life skills enabling function as an adult in the health-care system.

Seventh – Stop Micromanagement

Micromanagement occurs when payers and policy makers seek to implement a global or umbrella plan by controlling small details. It is defined well on *AZcentral.com*: "Micromanagement is the act of controlling every aspect of how another employee performs specific tasks or his role. This style of management does more harm than good to any organization. It suggests that a manager either doesn't trust an employee or doesn't have faith in her ability to do a job."[202]

Unfortunately, the goals and visions of health-care payers and policy makers may differ from many of the goals and visions of patients and their physicians. Payers and policy makers tend to make global processes for populations of patients. Indeed, global plans tend to make process the goal rather than the benefit to a patient.

In health care, controlling the process means regulating health-care providers. One means for regulating physicians is requiring board certification for granting medical practice privileges. Mandating physician board certification as the process to control granting of professional privileges was assumed to result in a decreased patient death rate as the surrogate for quality health care. However, analysis of comparative data about outcomes showed a lack of mortality benefit by mandating physician board certification.[203] An opposing assertion suggests insistence on board certification to practice medicine is more about control of the health-care sector and associated profits than about demonstrable improvement in patient care.[204] Control of the health-care business processes though restricting professional privilege grants is used as a mechanism for reducing cost through influencing a provider to follow the grantee's rules.

Micromanagement of providers in health care is frequently done by government entities or government-empowered entities. Such government actions are the antithesis to advice from Theodore Roosevelt that "[t]he best executive is one who has sense enough to pick good men to do what he wants done, and self-restraint enough to keep from meddling with them while they do it."[205] Overcoming micromanagement by the government or other entity requires recognizing and addressing undesirable characteristics of micromanagement as noted by Professor Richard White.[206] He lists seven micromanagement characteristics: (1) excessively supervising projects with detailed instructions, (2) acting as a control freak, (3) declining to give credit to subordinates, (4) obsessing over meaningless details, (5) creating arbitrary deadlines, (6) failing to finish projects, (7) and publicly abhorring mistakes as a justification for punitive actions.[207] Following Theodore Roosevelt's advice can eliminate these undesirable characteristics from health-care delivery by first assuming the physician and patient are capable of making and enacting medical decisions for the good of the patient. Instead of mandating adherence to nationwide population matrices, goals for individualized patient care and care processes can reasonably arise from the local medical-care community and patients.[208] In the same way, policing for failure in medical care because of negligence or incompetence should also be a local or regional process following the state's laws and regulations. As shown in the table below by James Beck, corporate directors, such as the government or payer, should direct while managers, such as caregivers, should manage.[209]

Table 1. Governance vs. Management Roles

Governance Roles	Management Role
• Govern the organization and act on behalf of the members in a "trustee" or "stewardship" role and are held accountable for the success or failure of the organization • Work 'on' the organization (as directors) with their hands firmly on the tiller, not in the engine room • Set the strategic direction and maintain control of the organization as a whole ***Directors Direct***	• Deal with the complexity and details of the day-to-day business operations and individual operational functions • Work in the organization (as managers represented by the CEO) • Act within the framework of the strategic direction and policies established by the board ***Managers Manage***

Changing micromanagement by government and health insurance payers also necessitates a change in behavior of the payers. An example for improving government management and micro-management has been addressed for other sectors under federal government control. An illustration is the recommendations for rescuing the United States Postal Service. Congress has been advised to repeal micromanagement-type mandated requirements and promote long-term goals.[210] That is, the government and other payers should provide a framework for the health-care industry while monitoring progress in fulfilling long-term goals for health-care provision. Formulating long-term goals should include input from providers and patients. Expertise of all involved parties would then be used. Making payments, an expertise of the United States Treasury, should be tied to the long-term treatment goal rather than an event in the treatment process. However, paying for health-care services should not be assumed to confer expertise in providing that service.

Eighth – Hospitals and Facilities

Some incentives causing the hospital lobby to seek more fee-for-service payment stems from a need to cover the cost for buildings and equipment. In the United States, hospital debt for nongovernmental institutions was $127.4 billion in 2007.[211] Increase in debt since that time is reported to be 30 percent in 2011 for the state of Connecticut.[212] While the most recent tax law allows for special section 179[213] and bonus depreciation,[214] the dollar amounts remain small compared to the total hospital debt. Fixed-structure debt remains high for hospitals.

Health institution financial stress is worsened by the high cost of labor for hospitals. This expense usually exceeds 50 percent of revenue.[215] Labor costs are variable but have fixed components, such as differential payment for night shift work. Furthermore, total labor expense tends to increase annually. Because twenty-four-hour service is necessary for most health-care facilities, hospitals are forced to maintain costly personnel rolls for adequate staffing. To provide needed cash flow for staffing, the hospital lobby has successfully persuaded payers, especially the federal government under the Medicare system, to increase payments for hospital-based services, whether as inpatients or outpatients. These hospital-based payments are often 50 percent higher than payments for the same services outside of the hospital system.[216] While health-care facilities have endeavored to shift services from the inpatient to outpatient designation, billing of these procedures remains based on inpatient fee schedules. Furthermore, flexibility to innovate care has been restricted by the mindset of corporate leaders, costs of buildings, costs of labor, and costs to satisfy regulations for an outpatient system. Expense reductions, in turn, are sometimes achieved for the inpatient payee, such as a health-care facility, by reducing hours of outpatient operation while the payers continue to pay inpatient rates for such work. These payments for outpatient services retire building debt and subsidize labor costs for the inpatient part of the business. This situation increases the tendency to build more facilities and facility space for continuing billing under the hospital-system payment system. However, more facilities and facility space necessitate increased staffing selected from a limited or shrinking pool of adequately trained people who, following economic principles of supply-and-demand, are paid increasing wages. Hence, the hospital lobby is incentivized to increase medical billing to cover increasing cost of doing business and building facilities. In turn, doing business and building facilities tend to increase medical billing.

Nevertheless, increasing flexibility of health-care facilities may innovate better care while controlling or reducing costs. Changing the health-care mission begins with changing the economic orientation of managers of such facilities. Removing the onus of debt and refocusing staffing to meet the desired patient services, outcomes, and locations should allow health-care facility managers and staff to fully participate in medical care innovations. Regulations and laws concerning health-care facilities would need reformation to address debt, imposed staffing requirements, and flexibility about repurposing facilities. Then, focus can be centered on the patient regardless of health service location. A benefit of the change in focus would be elevation of the individual patient outcome based on the patient's goals as a measure for success rather than financial spreadsheets and arbitrary, committee-determined clinical goals.

To remove the debt effect on medical decisions, a federal law would need to be passed that allows health-care facilities to expense debt payment each year. The Tax Cuts and Jobs Act of 2017 allows bonus depreciation of 100 percent for qualifying assets through the year 2022[217] but would need amending to specifically address medical facility investments. However, debt relief must be reciprocated by lobby activity relief trying to increase payments beyond inflation effects on costs. In return for being able to pay debt more quickly as an operating expense, participating facilities, systems, and health care corporations should agree to subsequently forego all federal lobbying concerning Medicare payments for seven years or the duration covered by the statute of limitation law. Failure to abide by the no-lobbying agreement would result in rescinding the debt expensing for income tax purposes to be replaced by a thirty-year depreciation. In addition, 20 percent of the claimed expenses would be payable as a fine to the federal government. Benefit from the government should not exclude benefit for improving the total cost of health care in America.

Part of the hospital expenses reflect mandated staffing. Federal and state staffing requirements should be lifted to allow the health-care facilities to find the best staffing mixes for their patient populations and scope of patient care. In return for removal of legislated micro-management of health-care staffing, health-care providers would participate in validated patient outcome and satisfaction surveys. That is, all surveys eligible for publication would first undergo peer-reviewed scientific evaluation. These patient outcomes and satisfaction reports would be publicly published in an ongoing basis with impartial explanations for public consumption. Explanations would also include comments from the facility regarding quality improvement efforts, optimizing staffing patterns, and responses to patient complaints. Rationale for staffing decisions would be included in these facility comments. Thus, rather than staffing to a legislator or bureaucrat idea, staffing mixes could change to allow evaluation of best practices for disease management and promotion of patient satis-faction. Performance measures would need continual reassessment for validity regarding treatment outcomes and patient-specific goal achievements. The results could be amalgamated to inform specific disease management. Those facilities where three-year performance remained more than 20 percent below the median performance by similar facilities would lose the eligibility to participate in annual funding for that managed population until deficiency remedies are verified. Thus, financial incentives would align with freedom to innovate while carrying a penalty for persisting health-care failure.

However, some facilities may choose to focus on specific chronic disease or health maintenance while opting out of care concerning other chronic disease or health-maintenance situations. Innovation in staffing patterns can therefore be tailored to the specific disease. Indeed, staffing for focused care has been effective for cancer when focus centers on care for patients with cancer rather than on cancer alone. In 2006, focused-care hospitals, called specialty hospitals, were found to have a lower mortality rate and higher patient satisfaction rate than community hospitals.[218]

Health-care facilities deal with debt and micromanagement regulations that constrain the activities and culture of each facility. If management of high debt burden, requirement to follow nonmedical, commercial business rules, and restriction to comply with micromanagement regulations were lifted, the health-care facility could truly focus on individualized patient care. Patient care provided by such health-care facilities would likely satisfy the desires of the patient as expressed through the doctor-patient relationship. Minimally, the desires of patients would be established as an important factor in health-care spending decisions by changing the focus of those decisions.

Ninth – Pharmaceutical Industry

Pharmaceutical cost, innovation, and supply have become a major concern in the United States. As explained in the Drug and

Therapeutics Committee Training Course handout from 2008, total cost of drug therapy includes procurement of the drug, personnel costs of handling the drug, and equipment costs for administering the drug.[219] The Belk article in 2018 reports revenue allocation by thirteen pharmaceutical companies included research (17 percent), profit (19 percent) and marketing (27 percent). The other 37 percent of revenue covered cost of business. Such allocations help determine the drug price. However, the price of a drug may also reflect the manufacturing company's desires to maintain revenue in an era when generic medication has become widely available.[220] Thus, many factors other than direct manufacturing costs affect the commercial price of medications.

Forty-five percent of the global pharmaceutical revenue came from sales in the United States.[221] Drug pricing also increases annually in the United States with a 13.1 percent increase occurring in 2014 for all drugs.[222] Some of the price increases anticipate loss of revenue as the medication faces generic competition. Pricing of generic drugs has generally affected pharmaceutical company revenue from 2010 to 2015 with most of the 1,441 established generic drugs having decreased prices from the brand drug. However, 315 established generic drugs' prices increased by more than 100 percent during those years.[223] Some of the price increases occurred when older generic medications were restudied, stimulated by the Unapproved Drugs Initiative put forth by the Food and Drug Administration in 2006. For example, colchicine, a drug used for gout and isolated in 1833, was restudied and changed from generic to brand-name, resulting in the per-pill price rising from $0.09 to $4.85.[224] In general, however, the business reasons for drug pricing remain closely held and unavailable to the public.

Price increases for medications have effects on patient compliance, leading to a public outcry for changes in pharmaceutical regulations. In Canada, high medicine prices led to noncompliance by about 10 percent of the patients. Low income, unhealthy, and uninsured patients were disproportionately represented in the noncompliance group.[225] Proposed solutions in the United States include instituting a single-payer system and Congressional-mandated price controls to control pharmacy expense. However, the Canadian experience with a governmental single-payer system covering "private" health care apparently has controlled these expenses by reducing health-care quality.[226] That is, Canadian government price controls reduced availability or use of medical services and medications.

In the United States, another frequent proposal to reduce drug costs suggests increasing market competition through developing generic drug supply as articulated by United States Food and Drug Administration (FDA) Commissioner Scott Gottlieb.[227] The World Health Organization issued a statement in 2017 that agrees with the FDA Commissioner that "a competitive marketplace is the best way to ensure low prices for medicines."[228] Control of drug prices has become a discussion point about health-care costs but is not the only issue regarding pharmaceuticals.

United States-based drug research investment in 2014 was over 37 percent of total drug research spending in the world.[229] From 1998 to 2007, about 47 percent of new drugs came from the United States.[230] Only 30 percent of potential new medications produce revenues exceeding research costs, as reported by Abbott and Vernon. Their 2005 paper concluded, using a few empiric studies and mathematical analyses, that drug research funding will fall if pharmaceutical company revenue falls.[231] A similar conclusion was reached by the RAND corporation in 2008.[232] Lim, in a comparison of patents granted to the semiconductor industry and the pharmaceutical industry, concluded that new drug patents depend on both basic and applied research as contrasted with semiconductor patents depending more on applied research.[233] Basic science research in the pharmaceutical industry does not directly produce revenue-generating products. Therefore, Lim averred continued funding through sales of old and new medications if innovation in medical care remains a goal for American health care.

Manufacturing is another issue affecting pharmaceutical pricing. Industry consolidation has been worldwide as seen with the Israeli company Teva Pharmaceuticals, which became the largest generic medication producer by acquiring competing companies. For many generic drugs, Teva Pharmaceuticals is a sole producer. Single-source drug production is not the only strategy for pharmaceutical companies to control the profit-loss balance sheet. Cost of labor influences the site for placing a manufacturing plant into low-wage cities. Companies that locate in low-wage cities may face natural or political problems, as seen in Puerto Rico after Hurricane Maria. About fifty manufacturing plants in Puerto Rico were damaged by Hurricane Maria, including the sole sources of thirteen medications.[234] Higher prices may reflect fewer manufacturing plants through reducing competition or natural disaster.

Another manufacturing issue affecting price is the mandated regulation of drug manufacturing safety by the FDA.[235] Inspectors must certify the production plant before any medication, including generic medication, can be sold in the United States. Drug manufacturing requires capital investment, initial licensing, and passage of subsequent inspections to protect quality and safety of the medication. Increased production capacity is desired by consumers while companies are required to maintain quality assurance for product safety before increasing production. All these issues require inclusion of production costs and cost-of-regulation compliance into the budget. Generating revenue to support the pharmaceutical industry requires successful analysis of the net future value for researching a new therapy, producing the proprietary medication, and future transition to generic production of medication.

In short, balancing cost, innovation, and production within the pharmaceutical industry can best be done by increasing competition within the industry while aligning regulations affecting expenditures and profitability from innovation to meet the goal of producing better medications. Accomplishing these goals remains a challenge. Research cost and initial profit must be preserved, which is done through the patent system. While the patent system must be respected, modification is needed to encourage developing new medications rather than the new packaging of old medications. Repurposing or proving the benefit of older generic drugs must be done without allowing "sticker shock" of abruptly higher prices. Perhaps the company repurposing an older generic drug could be awarded licensing fees for the life of the amended patent on the old medication. More importantly, generic medication production must conform to high standards to protect the patient while licensing and inspections must also be streamlined to allow more competition.

Finally, recognition is needed that the pharmaceutical industry differs from consumer goods manufacturing. Contrasted with consumer goods, most medications require prescription by a licensed practitioner for a patient of record in that medical practice. Prescription medications generally are not a consumer good used to produce personal satisfaction. Consumer direct advertising increases demand for a medication outside of the doctor-patient relationship. This Madison-Avenue-generated demand is counterintuitive when the doctor-patient relationship should focus to produce quality care. As opposed to the usual advertising purposes, demand for a prescription medication does not equate to appropriateness of that medication for the patient's disease. Indeed, as defined by Sachin Jain, advertising is used to create desire to buy something: "Advertising is undertaken by organizations in order to attract the attention of people towards products and services. Thus, the basic aim of advertising is to create awareness in the minds of people about the availability of products and services and influence them to buy the same."[236]

Thus, advertising of medications to the general population ignores both the doctor-patient relationship and the complex decisions about health care made through that relationship. Curtailing advertising generation of demand for a drug may reduce overall pharmaceutical expense and help reduce stress on the doctor-patient relationship. Belk reported marketing as 27 percent of the business expense for the pharmaceutical industry in 2018.[237] Advertising by pharmaceutical companies should not be allowed as a business deduction unless the message is an educational activity for the health-care provider or the patient alongside the health-care provider. Monitoring pharmaceutical advertising can be done by the Food and Drug Administration to keep language consistent with the drug package insert. The pharmaceutical industry must be refocused on providing treatment options, including new therapies, directed by physicians for the benefit of their patients.

— SIX —

How to Go – Action Points

M
any improvement plans fail to be enacted because a disconnect exists between the desired outcome and the process necessary to reach that outcome.[238] Changing American health-care mentality from an acute-care process, fee-for-service system to a long-term health-and-disease management system that economically rewards all participants will be a daunting task. Transition from the current system to the new paradigm requires intelligent planning and definitive action, avoiding disruption of medical care, and delay implementing the new health-care structure. Such disruptions and delays would undermine the entire health-care reform process. Changes would need to affect (1) federal law, (2) state law, (3) professional conduct and mindset, (4) education for health-care providers, (5) education for patients, (6) repurposing health care facilities and systems, (7) pharmaceutical industry revision, and (8) new payment systems.

Federal Law

Multiple federal laws affect the practice, business, ownership, and innovation of medical care. Repealing or amending multiple laws is needed to allow a new practice and business model providing medical care that also enhances the doctor-patient relationship. Laws to be changed include but are not limited to: (1) Consolidated Omnibus Budget Reconciliation Act of 1985:[239] The law prohibits federal demonstration projects covering competitive bidding for laboratory services. The law directs the Secretary of Health and Human Services (HHS) to regulate reasonable charges for physicians participating in Medicare. The law denies an income tax deduction for employees contributing to a group health plan not specified by the federal government. However, the law requires availability of continued health insurance after an employee leaves a job if that person pays the premium. (2) Omnibus Budget Reconciliation Act of 1990:[240] The law mandates a reduced reimbursement for new physicians over the first four years of practice. The law has multiple micromanagement provisions affecting health care. The law directs the Secretary of Health and Human Services to develop a system for federal review of individual physician activity outside the state medical boards. The law prohibits state Medicaid programs from using drugs not covered by a manufacturer's rebate program. The law required medication review and intervention by the pharmacist to establish pharmacy eligibility to receive Medicaid payment. This intervention was required as a search for drug abuse. (3) Omnibus Budget Reconciliation Act of 1993: The law mandates amortization over fifteen years for intangibles for patents, including drug patents which last seven years. (4) Healthcare Information Portability and Accountability Act of 1996:[241] The law allows medical conditions beginning six months before the insurance date to exclude eligibility for insurance for twelve months. However, the law prohibits excluding individuals from group health plans based on health status or medical condition. The law authorizes spending almost $1 billion for fraud and compliance investigations as part of the health-care budget. The law limits eligibility for a medical savings account to participants enrolled in a high-deductible health insurance plan.

(5) Medicare Prescription Drug, Improvement and Modernization Act of 2003:[242] The law limits cost coverage for prescription drugs, creating what is called the doughnut hole. The law limits funding the HSA to persons with a high-deductible health insurance policy. (6) Medicare Improvements for Patients and Providers Act (MIPPA) of 2008:[243] The law micromanages content of initial preventive health visits, including end-of-life planning regardless of the patient age or situation. The law mandates a bundled payment for dialysis service in lieu of any other payment. The law exempts Medicaid rules for specific localities in California. (7) American Recovery and Reinvestment Act of 2009:[244] The law incentivizes physician compliance with meaningful use of electronic medical records. Meaningful use means purchasing and installing health-care record software certified by the federal government, exchanging medical information via that software, and reporting various measurements to the federal government via the software. Hospitals also received incentives for conformation to meaningful use of electronic health records. (8) Patient Protection and Affordable Care Act of 2010:[245] The law micromanages as shown by defining the length and font size for insurance benefit explanation booklets. The law empowers the Secretary of Health and Human Services to annually review health-insurance premium increases for reasonableness. However, response to declared unreasonable rate increases was limited to lobbying the state to decertify the insurer. The law sets a $1 per covered life penalty against health insurers who fail to adopt electronic platforms complying with Health and Human Services regulations. (9) Food and Drug Administration Safety and Innovation Act of 2012:[246] This law mostly funds the Food and Drug Administration via fees imposed on drugs and medical devices. The fee schedules impose regulations on the respective manufacturers. Foreign pharmaceutical manufacturing inspection by United States inspectors can be replaced with reports from the foreign country's inspectors. Shortages in drug supplies is only reported periodically to Congress

with intervention limited to facilitated approval for manufacturing. (10) Medicare Access and Children's Health Insurance Reauthorization Act of 2015:[247] This law continues fee-for-service physician payments while establishing the principle of changing payments based on governmental definition of meritorious performance by the physician. That is, the law directs the Secretary of Health and Human Services to monetarily influence physician activities for achieving third-party mandated cost control and outcome measurements. Decisions within the doctor-patient relationship are not considered by the law. While chronic disease management is mentioned in this law, payment is limited to a single physician and not a team. (11) The 21st Century Cures Act of 2016:[248] National Health Institute funding is a major intent of this law but includes micromanagement of research initiative details. The law also allows Food and Drug Administration approvals for drugs and medical devices to be based on minimal information. However, the law also enables state-of-emergency declarations to permit off-label use of medications during the emergency period. Improvement in quality care for patients was mandated through using electronic health records and financial penalties for physicians. Interoperability of electronic health records was mandated with adoption by software developers remaining optional. Barriers preventing exchange of electronic medical data were addressed in the law under advisement of the Office of Civil Rights within the Department of Health and Human Services as a possible civils rights violation. (12) Amendment of 1986 Code:[249] This law removes the penalty for lack of having a personal health insurance policy by setting the fine as 0 percent of income. However, the provision requiring the purchase of a personal health insurance policy remains. Finally, (13) Several Social Security Amendment Acts over many years.

The new comprehensive health-care law will need to cover multiple provisions:

1. Medicare plans will be amended to include a long-term health and disease management capitation (DMC) option described in Chapter 3. Beneficiaries, regardless of age, who enroll in this option will be allowed to fund an HSA while traditional or Advantage Medicare enrollees would continue ineligibility per current law. The HSA option would be an incentive to participate in the new disease-management program. Eventually, however, the HSA should become available to all Medicare and Medicaid beneficiaries. The goal is to increase patient influence over expenditures for health care which requires patient possession of money for health-care expense.

2. All disability-eligible Medicare plans will convert to the DMC option with associated HSA. For example, when patients on dialysis receive a disability-based Medicare plan, the patient would enroll in a DMC plan.

3. Health insurance plans would be based on free market competition principles, including purchaser needs. While state insurance regulations would monitor and regulate the health insurance companies, the plans would be sold to anyone not covered by the Medicare program.

4. Businesses would be able to expense all costs for DMC plans whether purchased from insurance companies or part of a corporate self-insurance program. However, self-insurance plans would maintain confirmation of structure, rules, and viability for easy inspection by appropriate regulatory agencies.

5. As DMC plans cover chronic care for health and disease, there will be, by definition, no preexisting conditions. Only

existing conditions would be used to determine the specifics
of the chronic care coverage.

6. Businesses would be able to expense the costs of employee
company-wide health insurance regardless of the style of the
plan. If the expensed policy covers all costs for any individual
in a company, all employees must have access to the same
coverage at the same price adjusted for number of persons
covered. That is, the goal is providing employer-based comprehensive health-care insurance, not to generate a tax that
creates disincentive for providing comprehensive coverage
for health-care costs.

7. Individual, nonemployee-based health insurance policy
owners would be able to deduct the cost for DMC plans on
income tax filings as well as contribute $5000 to the HSA,
adjusted annually for inflation. Other types of individual
health insurance costs would be deductible, but HSA contribution deduction would be limited to $4000 per person
per year. Therefore, the HSA would be tied to long-term
health care management.

8. Legal residents who use health-care resources and could
not afford health insurance or chose not to purchase health
insurance would be enrolled into Medicaid based on the
rules and regulations of the state of residence. However,
failure to meet the state eligibility requirements would divert
the person to a federal health-exchange-type plan initiated when health services are first used. Disqualification
for Medicaid and unwillingness to pay the fee-for-service
health-care bill would activate the safety net federal health
insurance exchange. That is, the person without insurance
coverage would be involuntarily enrolled into the federal

health exchange at time of initial engagement of health care. State legislators would be encouraged to pass laws to pay that premium by allowing the involuntarily enrollment into the plan while garnishing wages. However, federal and state law would need changing to allow federal administration of the federal health exchange in all the states.

9.CMMS would administer the federal health exchanges but not Medicaid programs. The Medicare tax for individuals subject to involuntary enrollment into a federal health exchange would increase 50 percent to help cover the costs of insurance until a different health insurance plan is obtained for a year.

10. Congress would establish a dictionary of software definitions for all data fields used in the health-care record. That is, the software architecture would be compiled and maintained by the Library of Congress. To receive Medicare certification for payment for services covered by Medicare, the electronic health record vendors would be required to use only the Library of Congress definitions for their software architecture.

11. Congress would require portability of the electronic health record from site of service to another site of service with encryption controlled by the patient and the patient's physician. That is, restricting access to patient data by a vendor, data repository site, or health-care provider would be illegal, subject to punitive fines and jail sentences for the perpetrators. Software vendors would not be allowed to hold patient data hostage if the provider changed the electronic health record system.

12. Congress would pass a law allowing health-care facilities and systems to expense for corporate income tax purposes capital debt payments in exchange for foregoing federal lobbying activities regarding Medicare fee schedules for seven years. Failure to comply with the ban on lobbying would result in an immediate payment of the due taxes on the expensed debt plus a 20 percent penalty and a permanent ban in Medicare participation.

13. Congress would amend the so-called Stark Law to allow physician-owned entity participation with DMC plans.

14. Anti-trust laws would be amended to exempt participants in the DMC program from liability under the Sherman Antitrust Act of 1890 and other federal laws. However, proven falsification of outcome data and other issues affecting participation eligibility would be prosecuted as a felony. Management team participants not convicted of a felony when members of the team are convicted would be subjected to real-time compliance monitoring for three years.

15. Medicaid payments to the states would consist of block grants for those states that choose to participate fully in the new paradigm of disease management. The size of the grants would be based on the state population augmented by a 20 percent increase on the first three grant years for states with average per capita income 10 percent below the national per capita income or worse.

16. The Secretary of Education would receive a grant of $100,000,000 for public education. The money would be earmarked for teaching people how to participate in patient-centered health care. Grants of $50,000 per education

program would cover enrollment for 200 people. Grantees would need to show an assessment of the target population needs followed by plans to address those needs. Population-appropriate tools to gauge success in reaching the teaching goals would need to be used. These goals would be modified by socio-economic status, education level, disabilities, morbidity load, and other factors. Success would be defined as reaching or exceeding 80 percent of the population-specific goals. For each successful program, the grant would be reauthorized annually.

17. Corporate income tax law would be amended so that advertising to the public regarding prescriptive items, other than information about pharmacy location, would not be deductible. However, education grants for providers, medical conferences, and patients with their providers would be deductible. The education grants would be certified as educational by the continuing medical education accreditation entities which monitor commercialization of the education process to insure transparent and truthful presentations.

States

State legislation would need to establish a conduit for receiving federal health-care monies while customizing the appropriate health-care system for that state's population. Recognizing that powers not specified by the Constitution to reside in the federal government remain with the individual states, federal block grants should be granted with broad guidelines about eligibility and goals for the targeted health-care services. However, micromanagement by the federal government would be prohibited. Federal and state roles in the health care system would be differentiated to avoid confusion from overlapping authority. Acknowledgement that state and federal government play different roles in health care may induce cooperation between state and federal governments for formulating new paradigms in health care. Using federal funds for disease management programs could evolve into the only option for the federal government funding while allowing the states freedom to enact legislation providing new ways for health-care payments, insurance, and management. Tying otherwise unrestricted block grants of Medicaid money to fully implemented, state-regulated, disease-management programs would likely allow the fifty states to act as fifty laboratories producing innovation in medical care.

State legislatures will need to enact laws to become eligible for the block grants:

1. New laws would allow portability of health insurance plans across state lines if the state's minimal requirements for insurance carriers are met. The assumption is that minimal requirements will be reasonable and apolitical. Medicaid plans would be honored for three months to allow enrollment into a new plan for the person who moves to another state.

2. Insurance laws and regulations would be changed to allow the block payments to provider teams for DMC plans covering one, two, or three years of medical service for Medicaid-eligible beneficiaries. Each state could regulate the duration of the block payment.

3. Insurance laws would be amended to allow involuntarily enrollment of an uninsured person into a federal health exchange plan upon initially accessing otherwise unpaid medical care. Cash-paying patients would not be subject to this enrollment. Medicaid-eligible patients would be enrolled

into Medicaid rather than the health exchange plan. The laws will also allow court judgment for garnishing wages to pay the premiums if the person becomes subject to involuntary health plan enrollment.

4. Laws and regulations forcing health-care staff composition would be rescinded with a requirement that the facility or practice prove, by generally acceptable measurements, success in preserving patient safety, desired patient outcomes and patient satisfaction equal or superior to median satisfaction for comparable populations. The desired patient outcomes would be based on common health outcome measurements weighed by the patient's health goals. That is, the decisions formulated within the doctor-patient relationship would establish what is measured. Failure to remedy inferior outcomes and satisfaction surveys within three years could result in a loss of licensure but not prohibition for relicensure. However, developing other methods to induce physician interest and proactive participation in chronic disease management would be encouraged. Within each state, formation of many virtual laboratories evaluating effective staff composition and methods to increase preservation of the doctor-patient relationship for decision-making may result in innovation of patient health care.

5. Certificate-of-need laws would be rescinded as such laws restrict marketplace competition.

6. State licensing of facilities would be strengthened for both the quality of inspections and timeliness of inspections. Inspections would seek, by statute, to educate and engage the facility in improvement processes. Annual or biannual conferences with both inspectors and facility staff would

seek to refine the licensing process and to spread successful practices and techniques. Inspection teams would have job evaluations based on successful engagement of the inspected personnel in improvement processes. New facilities would need to be inspected within six months of commencing operations or receive a license until inspection could be performed. Reinspections would be done every three years to address past concerns and to facilitate cooperation between the state officials and the health-care facilities for promotion of quality improvement processes. However, a separate inspection team, available on a rapid-response basis, would respond to plausible complaints and observations suggesting poor patient safety. That inspection team would also be available for facilities requesting help with improvement processes.

7. Malpractice awards would be limited to the medical costs accrued, reasonably expected future medical costs, including living costs with the chronic disease, and a punitive damage maximum of $250,000 per case. Included in the award would be money covering health insurance premiums over the expected duration for health recovery or chronic disease management.

8. State licensing fees would include $500 per individual practitioner and $15,000 per facility for a fund covering expenses for patients who choose arbitration instead of malpractice litigation. If malpractice insurance premiums decrease, these fees could be collected yearly from each practitioner and health-care facility. The fee amount assumes that licenses would last three or more years, depending on state law.

Professional Conduct and Mindset

This new medical economic system is dependent on a return to the traditional importance of the doctor-patient relationship. Both parties will need to refocus on that relationship and the responsibilities engendered by such a relationship. Health-care providers will have the additional responsibility to develop resource management skills and interpersonal relationship skills which comprise the Art of Medicine. Tying development of management and interpersonal skills to state licensure will force participation in activities that promote the doctor-patient relationship. Continuing education can help professional development but needs to be augmented by professional activities with both peers and patients.

1. Initial licensure would require attending one or more patient-centered ethics seminars. That is, attending courses and seminars that include patients who can articulate the patient perspective in the doctor-patient relationship. Professional ethicists would be used to supplement education without supplanting the articulate patient. Physicians already licensed would need to attend such a seminar, submit evidence for a patient-centric approach, or submit affidavits from patients confirming such a practice.

2. Licensure would require seminars or professional training in management of health-care resources, especially teaching cost-benefit analysis when utilizing limited healthcare resources. Attending medical business courses would satisfy this requirement.

3. Providers would be required to show participation in quality improvement processes, patient advocacy processes, and/or patient support processes. A minimum of twelve hours

a year would need reliable documentation for relicensure. Examples of participation include but are not limited to such activities as participation in hospital committees, clinic quality improvement committees, national forums for patient care, patient information programs, and free clinics.

4. Provider quality improvement participation could include attending certified seminars and continuing medical education about quality improvement processes, patient advocacy processes, and patient support processes to satisfy participation requirements with continuing medical education credits.

5. Board recertification should change from being based on a formal timed testing to a system of demonstrated continuing medical education with participation in the processes such as those listed in above points 2, 3, and 4.

6. An award system should be developed by the health-care industry to recognize individuals and health-care systems producing innovative long-term health and disease management as well as individuals who successfully advocate and perform patient-centered health care. After the initial three years using the DMC system, such awards could be given annually. Responsibility for selection and management of awards could be delegated to medical board certifying organizations, state professional organizations or national professional organizations. Monies for awards could come from health-care organizations, health-care business, health-care providers, patient advocacy groups, and government grants.

Education for Health-Care Providers

The last momentous change in medical education followed the publication of *Medical Education in the United States and Canada* by Abraham Flexner in 1910. Responding to that negative report about medical education, medical schools developed a professional faculty, often hiring accomplished physicians from private practice. Advancements in medical treatments was aided by the medical school's ability to bring together thought leaders in medicine while providing a venue to conduct research trials. However, restricting medical education to fewer institutions produced some unforeseen consequences. Since the 1910 Flexner report, medical education has slowly become both intellectually inbred, through hiring faculty members out of training programs, and political, influenced by the need to secure general funding and research grant awards. Medical innovation has been encouraged while becoming legal property of the medical institution by employee contract, not the person innovating. Primacy of training physicians has, at best, slipped to co-equal status with increasing hospital or university system revenues through securing more research funding and expanding faculty-staffed patient-care venues. Competition for obtaining a larger amount of health-care dollars fosters competition between departments of a medical school plus private practice caregivers outside the medical school. Private practitioners no longer view the medical school as supreme consultation for a patient but as competition for any patient. In the medical training institution, competition between medical departments contributes to a silo mentality of working alone for the patient care.

In practice, silo mentality means that only a piece of medical care is provided by each rounding service for a hospitalized patient. For example, the admitting team intern or resident may be the only physicians allowed to write usual medical care orders for the patient. Meanwhile, the surgical team might remain peripheral to care unless surgery is definitively needed. Other subspecialty physicians might write suggestions without actively changing medical care delivery. When the days assigned to the patient-care service are finished, the caregivers change, including faculty physicians, which interrupts the opportunity to complete disease management and form the doctor-patient relationship. A shift-work mentality can develop, which seems to be validated by formal limits on trainee workload. That is, the trainee must stop the day's work after a certain number of hours or seeing a certain number of new patients. The silo and shift-work mentality can inhibit preparation of doctors to render long-term health and disease management.

Preparation to provide long-term care for a patient's health and disease requires adapting educational goals by changing the patient-care concept used in the teaching hospital and associated clinics. The mindset needs to change focus to a team-based care and long-term care perspective. Attaching conditions to federal money supporting post-graduate medical training may provide impetus for changing the training process and focus. Federal training grants could be increased 20 percent for institutions that make the following changes in training:

1. Mandatory weekly seminars would become multidisciplinary with the leader rotated among the various departments and divisions. For example, a talk about multivessel coronary artery disease would include the cardiologist, cardiovascular surgeon, nephrologist, physical therapist, intensive-care nurse and pharmacist, and other individuals with the thoracic surgeon leading the presentation. Another example is a presentation on femoral head (hip) fracture patients with the orthopedist as lead, supported by the hematologist, orthopedic nurse, physical therapist, and pharmacist.

2. Clinical research grants active in the medical schools would be monitored by a multidisciplinary team. The status and implications of clinical research would be routinely reported to the faculty and trainees. The process for doing clinical research would be a required teaching module for medical students, residents, and fellows.

3. Health-care training institutions would develop ongoing courses covering the business of medicine, including how to set up practice, cost-benefit analysis techniques, resource management, and the interaction between health care and the legal system. These courses would be provided for medical students, residents, and fellows.

4. Courses would be given that cover patient-centric ethics, processes for patient-centric continuing education, and logic for critical thinking.

5. In training hospitals, patient care would be done by teams with the leader of the team determined by the patient's primary active disease. Composition of the teams would be determined by the major emphasis of the service. As an example, a cardiac service would minimally include the cardiologist, pharmacist, nephrologist, endocrinologist, and rehabilitation specialist because diabetes is a common cause of complicated heart disease. Team rounding would be needed three times a week or more with contributions to care by all members of the team. Included in the team rounding would be time with the patient exploring the patient's goals and responses to treatment.

6. Outpatient clinics associated with medical schools would also utilize care teams tasked to develop processes delivering

efficient medical care for the large and complex outpatient population. A diabetic clinic would include an endocrinologist, primary care physician(s), nephrologist, ophthalmologist, pharmacist, and social worker/case manager. A cancer clinic would include an oncologist, infectious disease expert, pharmacist, social worker, oncology nurse, and hospice expert. A kidney clinic would include a nephrologist, endocrinologist, vascular surgeon, pharmacist, dialysis nurse, and a social worker/case manager.

7. Trainees would participate in team-building seminars during medical school and during post-graduate training.

Education for patients

Success in long-term health and disease management depends on the cooperation and participation of the patient. Unfortunately, Americans may reach adulthood publicly educated in sexual technique and gender issues yet lacking knowledge about body organ systems, consequences of decisions affecting health, resource management, and other basic adult decisions. Too many people leave public education without the basic reading and math skills needed for handling legal documents and bank accounts. Education can be achieved and education techniques can be tested through a grant program controlled by the Secretary of Health, Education, and Welfare.

1. Fifty-thousand-dollar grants would be given to public school systems, private schools, civic organizations, churches, teaching companies, and private entities who agree to comply with the grant provisions.

2. Each grant would pay for a program for twelve months.

3. Programs would use teaching techniques appropriate for the general learning characteristics of the target group. The students would be instructed in the following subjects:

    a. The anatomy and organ function, including organ location and health related issues.

    b. Effects of obesity, smoking, sedentary lifestyle, use of illicit drugs, and overuse of prescription drugs on the body contrasted with effects of following the currently accepted healthy lifestyle.

    c. Legal documents needed by adults including identification cards, wills, power of attorney, and advanced directives.

    d. Basic math to handle checking accounts and health savings accounts.

    e. Techniques for making and voicing one's health-care goals.

    f. Techniques in making decisions that require choosing between alternate therapies.

4. Eligibility to repeatedly receive the grant would depend on reporting verifiable data documenting teaching results for 150-200 people (that grant pays a minimum of $250 per person) and confirmation of achieved learning goals by 80 percent or more of the people in the class. The measurement parameters assessing learning would be adjusted for the abilities of the population taught. Success measurements would include percentages of the class completing legal documents, handling financial accounts, and formulating health-care goals.

5. Every two years, grantee performance would be assessed regarding achievement of standardized goals while adjusting for flexible techniques geared to the target population. Failure to develop a reproducible, effective learning system after participating in the program for two years would remove that program from grant eligibility for two years.

Repurposing Healthcare Facilities and Systems

Inflexible health-care facilities promote stagnant thinking about health care. Indeed, bricks and mortar tend to constrict thinking about health-care services as being attached to the bricks and mortar. However, buildings are needed, including offices for providers. A physician or a nurse, for example, usually requires a place to think, complete medical records, read, write, and rest. Having office space also contributes to the attitude of ownership of the health-care process. However, economic stress can be reduced by avoiding diversion of much capital into cosmetic upgrades, larger building funds, and increasing rents rather than treatment process development. Repurposing a facility and system can be difficult as such purpose may frequently change while the building debt remains. Allowing increased flexibility with health-care facilities will need several processes:

1. Payment of facility debt should be deemed an expense for income tax purposes. Eligibility to use this tax provision would occur with signing an agreement to not engage in lobbying the federal legislature regarding hospital payment amounts over a period covered by the current tax statute of limitation. Other forms of lobbying that did not affect hospital payments would be allowed. Violating the agreement would disallow use of that expense for that tax year. An additional penalty would be an additional 20 percent of

the due tax plus interest per year based on prime interest plus 1 percent.

2. Payments for medical services, other than the DMC system, would not be location based such as in a hospital, hospital-owned non-hospital building, urban setting, or state. That is, payment for fee-for-service activity would be based on the service provided rather than the site of service.

3. The diagnosis-related group (DRG) payment system would be continued and updated. Hospitals would have the option to accept an annual capitation payment based on prior Medicare payments for the managed disease rather than DRG payments.

4. Facilities and systems with annual patient care outcomes more than 20 percent better than the median outcome for the discharge diagnosis would receive a 10 percent bonus for traditional Medicare payments. The annual outcomes would be compared to the median outcome from prior years 2 through 4.

5. For participating in the DMC system, that facility would be allowed to establish a medical home partnering with a physician team leader for that disease process. This provision would encourage medical schools and associated hospital systems to participate in the DMC system.

6. Federal and state laws, with associated regulations, would be changed to allow inpatient facility participation in outpatient care paid at the outpatient rate. Like removing the concept of preexisting disease, this change would remove consideration

of the site for best payment when rendering medical care when picking the best location for a health service.

7. Certification and licensing processes by states and the federal government would change emphasis to facility maintenance, safety success, and patient-centric care rather than to regulating processes that might be site specific.

Pharmaceutical Industry Revision

The pharmaceutical industry needs to be reengaged as a component in American medical care for disease management and removed from a commercialized consumer products industry. The industry is not the evil Mr. Hyde as described by the Wellness Directory of Minnesota, which states, "[the] pharmaceutical industry is an example of the worst parts of capitalism, capitalism at its least respectable low and capitalism at its most ludicrous high."[250] Neither is the pharmaceutical industry a provider of the "right to health" "doing no harm and doing good" as averred by Klaus M. Leisinger.[251] Hyperbole about the industry needs to be set aside to allow, under judicious regulatory and legislative rules, incentives for finding new medical therapies with reasonable profitability while eliminating economic tyranny over a captive purchasing population.

Legislative and executive control over the pharmaceutical industry is mostly federal in the United States. Regulation by the United States government should amend the following laws and enforcement mechanisms:

1. Patent laws should be enforced internationally for new medications. Effective enforcement requires multinational treaties or agreements, especially defining the duration of patent

protection. Violating patent protection must carry stiff, enforceable penalties.

2. Generic and biological equivalent medications would need to perform within 10 percent of the standard established for the patented drug. However, research producing 25 percent improved drug performance would confer eligibility for a new or revised patent on the improved form of the drug lasting seven years. The Food and Drug Administration would judge eligibility for the patent change.

3. The duration of patent protection for a new class of medication should be based on commercially reasonable time to recoup developmental costs. That is, the patent application would detail costs for research and development. Duration of patent protection could be set from ten to fifteen years but would remove that drug's eligibility to be covered by a new patent based on new packaging or combination with other standard medications. The intent is to avoid inflicting unaffordable costs on the patient during the time of drug patent protection.

4. Patent protection for manufacturing and marketing could be extended ten years if the patent holder licensed generic medication production to be sold at a 30 percent or more lower price during the duration of the initial patent.

5. Both the Act of July 2, 1890 (Sherman Anti-Trust Act), which prohibits amalgamating manufacturing to develop a monopoly, and the Clayton Act of 1914, which prohibits price-fixing and noncompetitive bidding, would be enforced regarding generic drug manufacturing to ensure multiple sources for that medication. The FDA would be used to

monitor and enforce the quality and capacity of diversified generic drug manufacturing.

6. The Medicare Prescription Drug, Improvement, and Modernization Act of 2003 would be amended or replaced to allow both the Medicare and Medicaid programs to negotiate prescription drug prices for beneficiaries.

7. Tax laws and regulations would be changed, prohibiting consumer advertising costs as corporate income tax expense. Instead, covering costs for provider and patient education without commercial bias would be a business expense if such activities were conducted under the aegis of an organization that certified continuing medical education activities was without commercial bias.

8. The FDA would receive budgeted monies of $1 billion a year to fund national and international inspectors for pharmaceutical manufacturing plants. These inspectors could also select up to ten international factories, organizations, or individuals per year for $1 million awards based on innovation in manufacturing safety, product packaging safety, worker safety, or success in producing an "always right – never wrong" manufacturing process. Eligibility for the award would be limited to companies selling 50 percent of their product in the United States or supplying ≥ 50 percent of a medication for the United States market.

New Payment Systems

At first glance, this proposed change in medical economics seems to promote a single payer system. However, the single payer system would be the antithesis to maintaining medical decision control within the doctor-patient relationship. A single-payer system would necessarily tend to make autocratic decisions. Single payer decisions would tend to inhibit innovation in medical care while multiple payers would have more flexibility for innovation. However, a medical insurance system focused on fee-for-service remains economically unsustainable. Instead, the health insurance industry market needs to be transformed in focus.

While insurance plans could include traditional individual plans, new plans modified for a disease management strategy are needed. Group plans could be diversified to allow limited coverage, fee-for-service coverage, or health and disease management. Corporate self-insurance modified for employee satisfaction could also be encouraged. Plans for corporation self-insurance could be tailored for the kinds of employees hired by that corporation. Separate catastrophic insurance coverage would become more adjunct for all insurance plans. Several general insurance needs must be addressed by legislation:

1. Preexisting conditions no longer exist as a definition. The existing condition would determine the insurance plan coverage obtained. Healthy individuals may choose a traditional POS-type plan while individuals with a chronic disease would be funneled into a DMC-type plan.

2. Employment-generated health insurance would become portable. Changing jobs would allow existing insurance coverage to remain for remainder of the year. Any increased cost for keeping the old plan, compared to the new employer's

plan, would be paid by the covered individual. If the person became unemployed, eligibility to continue existing health insurance at that person's expense would continue.

3. Changing to a new employer's health insurance would be seamless, without a wait or vesting period, assuming the covered individual completes any probationary employment requirements.

4. Catastrophic insurance plans would be portable without change in premium unless all catastrophic insurance premiums for plans from that insurance company have been increased by the same amount.

5. DMC plans would be allowed to vary costs and coverage for that insurance product but not for the individual beneficiary. That is, a company could choose which disease to cover but not the individuals who have the disease. The Medicare DMC plan would provide the standard for disease management coverage. Federal and state statutes would establish the legal framework for the insurance plans and the standardization of coverage provisions. The Medicare DMC plan would set the standard for disease management plans. Failure to meet the Medicare standard would lead to loss of licensure for underwriting that type of health insurance until the deficiencies were remedied.

6. Beneficiaries would receive good outcome bonuses paid to the person's HSA if net savings on health-care costs occur through the management plans.

7. State laws would allow portability across state lines for plans that meet minimum state standards.

8. Prices for fee-for-service health care would be published by providers and insurance companies and include physician visits, laboratory studies, procedures, radiology tests, medical equipment, and prescriptions. Patients receiving fee-for-service health care would receive the prices upon enrollment into an insurance plan or initiating a health-care event for self-pay services. That is, health care providers accepting private payments will publish prices for common services.

9. Accounting firms, such as insurance intermediaries, for DMC plans would report status of the pools of money for each patient on a quarterly basis by a mailed or electronic statement. These reports would be delivered to the patient and all active providers. Real-time paperless accounting at a secure website would be analogous to banking and HSA websites.

— SEVEN —

Afterthoughts
in Times of COVID-19

The COVID-19 pandemic has altered American life while I am finishing this book. Clearly revealed are differences between government control of medical decisions versus patient-with-physician control of medical decisions. Government decisions differ from decisions produced within the doctor-patient relationship because the actions have different targets, that is, the general population versus the individual. The actions by government and corporations to deliver population care starkly differ from actions by patients and their physicians to deliver personalized medical care. That is not to say that centralized decisions and actions are invalid or unneeded. Indeed, centralized authorities are needed to track data, spur national response to manufacture needed resources and insure dissemination of those resources. Governments are also better equipped to track trends and respond to those trends with local, national, and global policies. However, such responses are less concerned with a particular patient-care process and more concerned with the end product or report about the end product. In contrast, individuals chose actions intended to produce a desired, individualized result. In a way, the differences between governmental and individual actions illustrate the difference between accepting that the ends justify the means versus accepting, for individualized health care, that the ends reflect the means.

Governments and, by extension, corporations make goal decisions regarding groups, or, in medical parlance, patient populations. Such decision-making is a top-down process formulating necessarily general goals. Goals are chosen to keep the majority of patrons or beneficiaries happy so that the government or corporation remains profitable regarding power or money. For a top-down process, the mechanism for achieving the goal is mostly limited to a process of allocation. In health care, government uses allocation to control supply of resources and distribution of resources. Olen Bruce's answer, intended for high school students, explains what government allocation means:

> The government can help influence the allocation of resources, or the ways in which producers have access to the means of production and the ways in which goods and services are distributed among consumers, in different ways. In a command economy, which is an economy in which the government controls which goods are produced, the government controls the allocation of resources based on their political needs and wants. In a capitalist or free market economy, the price system largely decides how resources are allocated or distributed among consumers and used. However, in a capitalist or semi-capitalist society, the government has the means to direct the allocation of resources. It can, for example, offer tax breaks or subsidies to private companies to produce needed goods and services, such as affordable housing or clean energy. In addition, the government can decide to offer these goods or services itself, such as building roads or hospitals, if the private sector does not do so.

Government and corporate decisions about supply and distribution of health care resources cover broad needs and, usually, are disconnected from individual health-care goals. However, all health-care resource decisions affect individual patients. How resource allocation decisions affect individual health care is illustrated by both ventilator supply and triage for ventilator usage during the COVID-19 pandemic.

In 2015, the State of New York published a report by the New York State Department of Health with the Task Force on Life and the Law assessing the state's preparedness for a pandemic of influenza. Ventilator availability was listed as 8,991 machines, of which 1,750 were in a reserve stockpile. However, only 2,836 machines would be immediately available for emergency use if influenza caused a surge in ventilator need. If a severe influenza pandemic occurred, that report estimated a peak need for 18,619 ventilators. Based on the 2015 inventory, the hospitals in New York State would be short 15,783 machines for emergency use. Resource allocation decisions from 2015 through 2019 did not address the projected shortfall in ventilators for the State of New York as revealed by the ventilator status report in March of 2020. As of March 25, 2020, New York State reported 4,000 ventilators in state hospitals with another 7,000 machines newly purchased for the state reserve. The federal government made available another 4,000 ventilators at that time. Thus, estimated shortage of predicted peak-need ventilators was 3,619 machines. This projected material shortage of resources led to speculation that rules were needed to allocate usage of possibly insufficient resources. In other words, a plan for rationing ventilators was thought to be needed.

Once the government or corporate decision is made allocating expenditures for stockpiles of emergency-use resources, occurrence of a crisis forces decision-making about how the reserved resources are utilized. That is, leaders in the government and corporations make decisions, sometimes under duress, about allocation of resources.

These top-down decisions are usually based on utilitarian principles. Utilitarianism views goals from a population perspective contrasted with a personal goal made within the doctor-patient relationship. Norman Fost presents a utilitarian perspective when writing for *Future Tense*, a partnership between Slate Group created by Donald Graham of the Washington Post, New America, which is a think tank in Washington, D. C., extensively funded by Bill and Melinda Gates, and Arizona State University. He writes:

> The first piece of this public education is to make clear that there must be a shift from the traditional ethical commitment to the interests and preferences of each individual patient, to a commitment to the interests of the community. In times of abundance, society can afford to offer a ventilator to a dying patient with little chance of survival, but not when another patient will die who had excellent prospects for a long life. … But if the guidelines are developed in an open way, with good faith efforts to consider the perspectives of the wider community, few people will disagree that it's better to have guidelines than to leave decisions to individual physicians.

Advocating this utilitarian allocation process also assumes that personalized decisions, regarding intubation and ventilation use in this case, run contrary to interests of the community at large. More importantly, the opinion offered in *Future Tense* assumes the ethics about rightness or wrongness of these medical decisions are best determined by public and political officials. However, as Nick Romeo wrote in an article for *Vox.com*, rationing or allocating medical care is the "grim ethical dilemma." While Mr. Romeo concludes that collective action to ration care will eventually reduce suffering by patients and providers, "American health care workers will likely face agonizing decisions on how to ration care." I argue that agonizing over decisions to ration care is desirable and should be done within the doctor-patient relationship.

Another consequence of such top-down decision-making is illustrated by what happened in New York State regarding translocation of COVID-19 patients. Based on models projecting an increasing number of critically ill COVID-19 infection cases, the State of New York determined that hospital resources would not meet that projected need. To empty hospital beds for anticipated needs, the New York Department of Health mandated, by a memo on March 25, 2020, the transfer from hospitals to nursing homes of patients with suspected or confirmed COVID-19 infection. The next day, March 26, 2020, the Associated Press, through the *Journal of Emergency Medical Services*, reported about 300 total New York State COVID-19-related deaths from the start of the pandemic. About a month later, on April 22, 2020, the *Daily Star* from Oneonta, New York, reported a new death count. That April 22 article reported the total New York State COVID-19-related deaths to be 15,302 people, of which 3,505 deaths occurred in nursing homes. The New York Department of Health mandate was made with three-week-old knowledge that COVID-19 severely affected a Washington State nursing home. In a single Washington nursing home, seven people died as the *New York Times* reported on March 4, 2020, thus informing medical officials that nursing home patients carried increased risk for dying when infected with COVID-19. An interesting graph from *Wikipedia*, using data from Johns Hopkins University, shows the New York State case fatality rate (CFR) abruptly increased twenty days after the New York Department of Health mandate of March 26. Twenty-two days after the mandate, the New York CFR was higher than the United States as a whole. It is clear that state- or corporate-mandated usage allocation during a medical crisis can have unintended but not necessarily unforeseen consequences. More importantly, when top-down decisions are made and enforced, an individual's life, liberty, and pursuit of happiness can be disregarded as irrelevant compared to the perceived good for the whole population.

The COVID-19 pandemic spotlights differences between centralized, non-personalized mandates affecting medical care and the individual actions modifiable through the doctor-patient relationship. Of course, a societal crisis, such as a pandemic, war, or natural disaster, necessitates temporary changes to an individual's habits and conduct, including medical care. Individuals need to act responsibly by applying government-supplied information and guidelines to secure the best situation for oneself, one's family, and one's friends. However, no global crisis management optimizes control of medical care and personal rights of the individual. Instead, a global crisis necessarily optimizes the power of the government over the governed. Looking back at the time following World War I, Steve Forbes stated: "In no country did governmental powers recede to prewar levels. They almost did in the US—until the Great Depression." If personalized, effective, and economically sound medical care is the desire of American citizens, then government and corporations are unlikely to support what is deemed unsuitable for the majority. Indeed, if the thinking of Norman Fost is embraced, individual health-care decisions must be subsumed by benefit for the whole group. However, if individualized medical care is to be maintained, the doctor-patient relationship must be rescued.

Rescuing the doctor-patient relationship from economic and pandemic problems found in the twenty-first century is a daunting challenge. The health-care industry is imploding from rising costs, reflecting increased utilization, inefficient utilization, administrative costs, regulatory costs, commercialization for nonmedical reasons, and costs for innovation. Addressing the problem by increasing regulation will likely worsen costs without personalizing care. Many times, increased regulations have the purpose of protecting what is officially designated as common good. However, the unintended consequence of increased regulation is adding administrative costs to medical care. The American Hospital Association estimated, in 2017, a $39-billion burden incurred for regulatory compliance for health systems, hospitals, and post-acute care facilities. These rising costs, forced by governing regulations, must be attenuated as one of the remedies to lessen growth in national health-care costs.

Using regulation to address rising health-care costs is actually a cosmetic change rather than a fundamental structural change. That is, regulations change appearance and associated processes of the health-care system. However, cosmetic changes to governance for American health care will eventually lead to failure of a historically successful health-care system. Cosmetic changes will not reduce influences and structural problems that continually increase the national cost of health care. Instead, structural changes are needed in how health care is paid and decisions made. As an initial change, the payment system incentives must also be realigned from control with a top-down system to control at the site care provision. Changing the monetary control site to cover health-care expense changes the payment process. More importantly, placing control of expenditures within the doctor-patient relationship changes the provision and costs of health care.

Why is this important? The doctor-patient relationship can focus regulatory and economic factors to enhance effective health care, especially if the resources and monies available are specified before care is given. Duplication of services and wasting money on treatments unlikely to provide the patient's desired results can be avoided. Unfortunately, the current trend in the health-care industry de-emphasizes the doctor-patient relationship as the provider of medical decisions and controller of spending. A fundamental change in both the regulatory and economic structure of American health care is needed in a way that preserves the doctor-patient relationship.

Failure to enact comprehensive change in American health care without preserving the doctor-patient relationship will eventually undermine the stability of our current medical system or obviate the individual's desired health-care product. A needed change in our current system is control over cash flow for medical care. Regulatory restrictions need to be changed from those that siphon monies to both administration and regulatory compliance. Moreover, the mantra "high-quality health care," which is an administrative and regulatory tool imposed by payers and regulators to reduce payments for services regardless of what happens at the point of medical service, should be replaced with "personalized high-quality health care." Producing a personalized high-quality health care process necessitates ownership involvement by both the physician and the patient. Ownership promotes reaching for the best outcomes within the specified budget. The current system without grassroots ownership has proven costly while producing results that have been criticized compared to the rest of the world. The daunting task is how to alter the current pathway of American medical care towards bankruptcy or the worse result of mediocrity.

Altering the future of the American health-care behemoth requires changing people and institutions. Changing attitudes and skills of patients and health-care providers will be a difficult task. Moreover, in comparison, reforming business and government bureaucracies seems to be impossible. However, failure to attempt reforming health-care business leads to a catastrophic outcome if the current economic and regulatory system continues. An inflexible system with increasing health-care costs remains unsustainable. However, current political and think-tank discussions seem to view problems with health-care funding as a monolithic issue. Discussions do not consider how increased demand for services, unanticipated consequences of legislation, micromanagement tendency of bureau-cracies, cost-cutting using service reduction as a business strategy for health-care corporations, and decreasing patient skills contribute to the developing chaos affecting the American health-care sector. Most importantly, calls to refocus the attention of health-care policy and regulation onto the patient through the doctor-patient relationship seem to fall upon deaf ears. In fact, despite stagnant and repetitious public discussions about the health-care system, challenging change is coming to health care regardless of our willingness or preparation to meet that challenge.

For those officials who prefer planning for populations, grouping patients desiring similar outcomes with similar disease and health status can be a basis for some clinical research and policy development. If patient desires regarding outcomes are included as a basis for clinical research study design, methods to individualize therapies may be learned. For those people who seek value-based health economics or measurement systems, new metrics can be developed based on patient desired outcomes over years rather than short-term outcomes needed for publication or pharmaceutical approval. This approach includes the patient as an owner-participant in the health care system. Eventually, patient goals and medical business goals could become aligned if the patient is viewed as a participant rather than a commodity.

Patient care and quality of that care remain based on the relationship between that patient and the physician. That relationship will continue despite the outcome of the developing economic chaos. Within that relationship, the patient needs to be taught the power of decision-making along with the health and economic consequences of those decisions. Eventually, the doctor-patient relationship can be used to focus economic, institutional, measurement, and innovation strategies for medical care. However, individualized long-term disease and health management also needs to be the goal of health services. Indeed, long-term disease management is basically a long-term relationship between people through the doctor-patient relationship. More importantly, through rescuing the doctor-patient relationship, the vision of Hippocrates to avoid harming the patient and actively promote the good for the patient can regain central importance for health care in America.

Endnotes

1 Maureen Buff and Timothy J. Terrell. "The Role of Third Party Payers in Medical Cost Increases," *Journal of American Physicians and Surgeons* (2014): 75-79.

2 OpenSecrets,org, *Top Industries*, October 29, 2019, https://www.opensecrets.org/lobby/top.php?indexType=i.

3 "Physician Patient Relationship Law and Legal Definition," *USLEGAL.com*, 2016. https://definitions.uslegal.com/p/physician-patient-relationship/.

4 Peggy Rothbaum, "The Doctor-Patient Relationship Is Everything," *KevinMD.com*, November 22, 2017, https://www.kevinmd.com/blog/2017/11/doctor-patient-relationship-everything.html.

5 Ibid.

6 Center for Disease Control and Prevention, "State HIV Testing Laws: Consent and Counseling Requirements," *CDC.gov*, March 15, 2015, https://www.cdc.gov/hiv/policies/law/states/testing.html.

7 Ibid.

8 Jonathan J. Kim, *Legal Information Institute*, May 2017, https://www.law.cornell.edu/wex/contract.

9 Valerie Blake, "When Is a Patient-Physician Relationship Established?" *AMA Journal of Ethics* (2012): 403-406.

10 H.M. Evans, "Do Patients Have Duties?" *Journal of Medical Ethics* (2007): 689-694.

11 "Good Samaritans Law and Legal Definition," *USLegal.com*, 2016, https://definitions.uslegal.com/g/good-samaritans/.

12 Cheryl Gutherz and Shira Baro, "Why Patients with Primary Care Physicians Use the Emergency Department for Non-urgent Care," *The Einstein Quarterly Journal of Biology and Medicine* (2001): 171-176.

13 American Medical Association, *Billing medicaid patients*, 1999, http://www.whatismedicalinsurancebilling.org/2009/10/billing-medicaid-patients.html.

14 Kayla Holgash and Martha Heberlein, *Health Affairs Blog*, April 19, 2019, https://www.healthaffairs.org/do/10.1377/hblog20190401.678690/full/.

15 Modern Medical Network, "Discounting Fees for Self-Pay Patients," *PhysiciansPractice.com*, February 1, 2008, http://www.physicianspractice.com/qa/discounting-fees-self-pay-patients.

16 Trisha Torrey, "Medicare's HCPCS Codes for Payments," *VeryWellHealth*, October 23, 2017, https://www.verywell.com/what-are-medicares-hcpcs-codes-2614952.

17 United States Government, "Rules and Regulations," *Federal Register* (2019): 9460-9463.

18 Kirk Raban, "Fair Market Value for Physician Compensation Arrangements," *Radiology Business Management Association*, Las Vegas Nevada, 2011.

19 *American Lithotripsy Soc. v. Thompson*, 215 F. Supp. 2d 23 (D.D.C. 2002). 1:01-cv-1812 (District Court, District of Columbia, July 12, 2002).

20 Maureen Buff and Timothy J. Terrell, "The Role of Third

Party Payers in Medical Cost Increases," *Journal of American Physicians and Surgeons* (2014): 75-79.

21 John Ashbaugh and Gary Smith, "Capitation and Risk Management," *Human Services Research Institute*, January 6, 1996, https://view.officeapps.live.com/op/view.aspx?src=https%3A%2F%2Fwww.hsri.org%2Ffiles%-2Fuploads%2Fpublications%2FMC103Capitationan-dRiskManagement.DOC.

22 Patrick C. Alguire, "Understanding Capitation," *American College of Physicians*, 2017, https://www.acponline.org/about-acp/about-internal-medicine/career-paths/residency-career-counseling/guidance/understanding-capitation.

23 John Ashbaugh and Gary Smith, "Capitation and Risk Management," *Human Services Research Institute*, January 6, 1996, https://view.officeapps.live.com/op/view.aspx?src=https%3A%2F%2Fwww.hsri.org%2Ffiles%-2Fuploads%2Fpublications%2FMC103Capitationan-dRiskManagement.DOC.

24 Lisa Zamosky, "Direct-Pay Medical Practices Could Diminish Payer Headaches," *ModernMedicine Network*, April 14, 2014, http://medicaleconomics.modernmedicine.com/medical-economics/content/tags/concierge-service/direct-pay-medical-practices-could-diminish-payer-h?page=full.

25 Concierge Medicine Today, *Concierge Medicine Today*, May 2017, https://conciergemedicinetoday.org/concierge-medicine-cost/.

26 Brent C. James and Gregory P. Poulsen, "The Case for Capitation," *Harvard Business Review* (2016): 102-111.

27 Bob Morrow, "Interaction of Insurance and Kidney Care" (presentation, Chronic Kidney Disease: A Deep Dive 2018, National Kidney Foundation, Houston, TX, May 18, 2018).

28 Sonal M. Sekha and N. Vyas, "Defensive Medicine: A Bane to Healthcare," *Annals of Medical & Health Sciences Research* (April-June 2013): 295-296.

29 Physicians Practice, *Physicians Practice*, July 1, 2005, http://www.physicianspractice.com/qa/billing-benchmarks.

30 Danielle F. Loeb, Ingrid A. Binswanger, Carey Candrian, and Elizabeth A. Bayliss, "Primary Care Physician Insights Into a Typology of the Complex Patient in Primary Care," *Annals of Family Medicine* (2015): 451-455.

31 Sheri Porter, "How Would You Describe a 'Complex' Patient?" *American Association of Family Practice*, September 18, 2015, https://www.aafp.org/news/practice-professional-issues/20150918patientcomplexity.html.

32 John Flannery and Geraldine Kurukchi, "Caring for Patients with Chronic and Complex Care Needs: The AMA Proposes a Better Way," *ama.com.au.*, Australian Medical Association, April 29, 2010, ama.com.au/media/care-patients-chronic-and-complex-needs-ama-proposes-better-way.

33 Gov.UK, *New Era of Education and Training for NHS Staff*, May 28, 2013, https://www.gov.uk/government/news/new-era-of-education-and-training-for-nhs-staff.

34 ECRI, "ECRI Institute's 21st Annual Conference The 'New' Complex Patient: The Shifting Locus of Care and Cost," *ECRI. org*, Novemberber 2014, https://www.ecri.org/Resources/Conference/The-New-Complex-Patient-Conference-Summary.pdf.

35 Danielle F. Loeb, Ingrid A. Binswanger, Carey Candrian, and Elizabeth A. Bayliss, "Primary Care Physician Insights Into a Typology of the Complex Patient in Primary Care," *Annals of Family Medicine* (2015): 451-455.

36 Michael A. LaCombe, "Teaching and Learning by Example," *Annals of Internal Medicine* (2018): 521-522.

37 National Education Association, *History of Standardized Testing in the Unitied States*, 2017, http://www.nea.org/home/66139. htm.

38 Robert Anthony, *UBM Medica*, 2010, https://www.roswellpark. org/partners-practice/white-papers/board-certification.

39 Center for Medicare and Medicaid Services, *ESRD Conditions for Coverage (CfCs) Final Rule Rollout*, August 28, 2008, file:///D:/My%20Documents/Patient%20Based%20 Medical%20Care/FAQsESRDRolloutFINAL082808.pdf.

40 Alexander T. Sandu, R. Adams Dudley, and Dhruv S. Kazi, "A Cost Analysis of the American Board of Internal Medicine's Maintenance-of-Certification Program," *Annals of Internal Medicine* (2015): 401-408.

41 Andrew M. I. Lee, "No Child Left Behind (NCLB): What You Need to Know," *Understood for All, Inc.*, 2018, https://www.understood.org/en/school-learning/your-childs-rights/basics-about-childs-rights/no-child-left-behind-nclb-what-you-need-to-know.

42 Sarah E. Holmes, "Standardized Testing and the No Child Left Behind Act," (paper, East Carolina University, 2009).

43 "Every Student Succeeds Act," *Wikipedia: The Free Encyclopedia*, June 18, 2018, https://en.wikipedia.org/wiki/Every_Student_Succeeds_Act.

44 Bradley Gray, Jonathan Vandergrift, Rebecca S. Lipner, and Marianne M. Green, "Comparison of Content on the American Board of Internal Medicine Maintenance of Certification Examination With Conditions Seen in Practice by General Internists," *Journal of the American Medical Association* (2017): 2317-2324.

45 John Hayes, Jeffrey L. Jackson, Gail M. McNutt, Brian J. Hertz, Jeffrey J. Ryan, Scott A. Pawlikowski, "Association between Physician Time-Unlimited vs. Time-Limited Internal

Medicine Board Certification and Ambulatory Patient Care Quality," *Journal of the American Medical Association* (2014): 2358-2363.

46 Alexander T. Sandu, R. Adams Dudley, and Dhruv S. Kazi, "A Cost Analysis of the American Board of Internal Medicine's Maintenance-of-Certification Program," *Annals of Internal Medicine* (2015): 401-408.

47 Kurt Eichenwald, "A Certified Medical Controversy," *Newsweek.com*, April 7, 2015, http://www.newsweek.com/certified-medical-controversy-320495.

48 R.M. Epstein and E.M. Hundert, "Defining and Assessing Professional Competence," *Journal of the American Medical Association* (2002): 226-235.

49 University of Ottawa, "What is Professionalism in Medicine?" *University of Ottawa Medicine*, 2017, http://www.med.uottawa.ca/Students/MD/Professionalism/eng/what_is_professionalism.html.

50 Lynne M. Kirk, "Professionalism in Medicine: Definitions and Considerations for Teaching," *Proceedings Baylor University Medical Center* (2007): 13-16.

51 Atul Gawande, *Being Mortal: Medicine and What Matters in the End* (New York, New York: Picador USA, 2014).

52 Edmund Pellegrino, "The Medical Profession as a Moral Community," *Bulletin of the New York Academy of Medicine* (1990): 221-232.

53 Ibid.

54 CMA Health Policy Consultants, *The Center for Medicare Advocacy*, 2017, http://www.medicareadvocacy.org/medicare-info/quality-of-care/.

55 U.S. Department of Health and Human Services, *Office of*

Disease Prevention and Health Promotion, November 9, 2017, https://health.gov/hcq/.

56 Sarah Brumley, "What Is Quality Assurance in Health Care?" *Chron.com*, 2017, http://smallbusiness.chron.com/quality--assurance-health-care-76135.html.

57 United States Government, "H.R.2 - Medicare Access and CHIP Reauthorization Act of 2015," *Congress.Gov*, 2015, https://www.congress.gov/bill/114th-congress/house-bill/2.

58 Eduardo Lacson, Jr., Norma Ofsthun, and J. Michael Lazarus, "Effect of Variability in Anemia Management on Hemoglobin Outcomes in ESRD," *American Journal of Kidney Diseases* (2003): 111-124.

59 Danielle Ofri, "Quality Medical Care," *New York Times*, 2017, https://danielleofri.com/quality-medical-care/.

60 Margaret Gerteis, Susan Edgman-Levitan, Jennifer Daley, Thomas L. Delbanco, editors, *Through Patient Eyes: Understanding and Promoting Patient-Centered Care* (New York, New York: Jossey-Bass, 1993).

61 Melissa Snell, "Baldwin IV," *ThoughtCo*, 2006. https://www.thoughtco.com/baldwin-iv-profile-1788372.

62 "A Short History of the National Sanitarium Association (NSA)," *nationalsanitarium.ca*, National Sanitarium Association, 2019, http://nationalsanitarium.ca/history.

63 Unknown, "Soldier and Physician," Museo Archeologico Nazionale di Napoli, *Murals from Pompeii, Italy*, Naples, Italy, 2013.

64 David K. Osborn, "Galen: Greatest Physician of the Roman Empire," *GreekMedicine.net*, 2015, http://www.greekmedicine.net/whos_who/Galen.html.

65 Joshua Mark, "Health Care in Ancient Mesopotamia," *Ancient*

History Encyclopedia, May 21, 2014, https://www.ancient.eu/article/687/health-care-in-ancient-mesopotamia/.

66 Christian Nordqvist, "A History Of Medicine," *Medical NewsToday.com*, 2012, http://www.medicalnewstoday.com/info/medicine/ancient-greek-medicine.php.

67 Medical News Today Editorial Team, "What Is Ancient Greek Medicine?" *www.medicalnewstoday.com*, January 5, 2016, https://www.medicalnewstoday.com/info/medicine/ancient-greek-medicine.php.

68 Arthur Fairbanks, "Pythagoras and the Pythagoreans Translated 1898," *Hanover Historical Texts Project*, June 2013, https://history.hanover.edu/texts/presoc/pythagor.html.

69 Joshua J. Marks, "Egyptian Medical Treatments," *AncientHistoryEncyclopedia.com*, February 2, 2017, http://www.ancient.eu/article/51/.

70 Cai Jingfeng, "A Historical Overview of Traditional Chinese Medicine and Ancient Chinese Medical Ethics," *Ethik in der Medizin* (1998): S84–S91.

71 Ibid.

72 Massoume Price, "History of Ancient Medicine in Mesopotamia & Iran," *IranChamber.com*, October 2001, http://www.iranchamber.com/history/articles/ancient_medicine_mesopotamia_iran.php.

73 Gerry Greenstone, "The History of Bloodletting," *BC Medical Journal* (2010): 12-14.

74 White McKenzie Wallenborn, "George Washington's Terminal Illness: A Modern Medical Analysis of the Last Illness and Death of George Washington," *The Washington Papers*, November 5, 1999, http://gwpapers.virginia.edu/history/articles/illness/.

75 David K. Osborn, "Galen: Greatest Physician of the Roman

Empire," *GreekMedicine.net*, 2015, http://www.greekmedi-cine.net/whos_who/Galen.html.

76 W.H.S. Jones, *Hippocrates: Vol 1.* (London: Harvard Univser-sity Press, 1923).

77 John Gregory, *Lectures on the Duties and Qualifications of a Physicians*, Charleston: Nabu Press, 2014.

78 Robert Baker, "The Eighteenth-Century," in *The Codification of Medical Morality*, eds. Robert Baker, Dorothy Porter, and Roy Porter (New York: New York: Kluwer Academic Pub-lishers, 1993), 93-98.

79 Melissa, "Doctors Aren't Actually Bound by the Hippo-cratic Oath," *Gizmodo.com*, November 15, 2013, https://gizmodo.com/doctors-aren-t-actually-bound-by-the-hippo-cratic-oath-1465044222.

80 Robert Orr, "Professional Oaths: History, Usage, Content and Changes," *Christian Medical and Dental Association*, March 1, 2009, https://www.cmda.org/resources/publication/tcd-spring-2009-professional-oaths.

81 Edmund Pellegrino, "The Medical Profession as a Moral Community," *Bulletin of the New York Academy of Medicine* (1990): 221-232.

82 Deborah Mitchell, "Look At The History of Health Insurance in America," *Emaxhealth.com*, September 21, 2009, https://www.emaxhealth.com/1275/72/33689/look-history-health-in-surance-america.html.

83 Blue Cross Blue Shield, *An Industry Pioneer: Leading the Way in Health Insurance*, 2019, https://www.bcbs.com/about-us/industry-pioneer.

84 Linda Gorman, *The History of Health Care Costs and Health Insurance*, Background Research Report, Wisconsin Policy Research Institute, Inc., 2006.

85 Blue Cross Blue Shield, *An Industry Pioneer: Leading the Way in Health Insurance*, 2019, https://www.bcbs.com/about-us/industry-pioneer.

86 Linda Gorman, *The History of Health Care Costs and Health Insurance*, Background Research Report, Wisconsin Policy Research Institute, Inc., 2006.

87 John Henning Shumann, "A Bygone Era: When Bipartisanship Led To Health Care Transformation," *National Public Radio*, October 2, 2016, https://www.npr.org/sections/health-shots/2016/10/02/495775518/a-bygone-era-when-bipartisanship-led-to-health-care-transformation.

88 Ken McDonnell, "History of Health Insurance Benefits," *EmployeeBenefitsResearchInstitute.org*, March 2002, https://www.ebri.org/publications/facts/index.cfm?fa=0302fact.

89 Health Insurance Institute, "Source Book of Health Insurance Data 1979-1980," Washington, D.C., 1980.

90 Rosemary Stevens, "Health Care in the Early 1960s," *Health Care Financing Review* (1996): 11-22.

91 Kimberly Amadeo, "The Rising Cost of Health Care by Year and Its Causes," *The Balance.com*, June 25, 2019, https://www.the-balance.com/causes-of-rising-healthcare-costs-4064878.

92 Social Security Administration, "Notes and Brief Reports," *www.sa.gov*, 1974, https://www.ssa.gov/policy/docs/ssb/v37n3/v37n3p35.pdf.

93 Clifton B. Perry, "What Standard for the Standard HMO Gatekeeper?" www.thefreelibrary.com, The Free Library, July 1, 2001, https://www.thefreelibrary.com/What+standard+-for+the+standard+HMO+gatekeeper%3f-a082881813.

94 Veronda M. Finley, "Patient Satisfaction in Managed Care," (master's thesis, University of Nevada, Las Vegas, 2001), *http://digitalscholarship.unlv.edu/thesesdissertations*.

95 "HMO vs PPO," *Diffen.com*, September 3, 2017.

96 United States Congress, "Title 42 / Chapter 7 / Subchapter XVIII / Part B / § 1395w-4," *uscode.house.gov*, March 26, 2020, https://uscode.house.gov/view.xhtml?req=granuleid:USC-prelim-title42-section1395w-4&num=0&edition=prelim#.

97 "2016 Survey of America's Physicians: Practice Patterns & Perspectives," www.physiciansfoundation.org, The Physicians Foundation, September 2016, https://physiciansfoundation.org/wp-content/uploads/2018/01/Biennial_Physician_Survey_2016.pdf.

98 IHS Markit Ltd., "The Complexities of Physician Supply and Demand: Projections from 2017-2032," *Association of American Medical Colleges*, April 2019, https://aamc-black.global.ssl.fastly.net/production/media/filer_public/31/13/3113ee5c-a038-4c16-89af-294a69826650/2019_update_-_the_complexities_of_physician_supply_and_demand_-_projections_from_2017-2032.pdf.

99 Robert M. Ball, *Social Security Amendments of 1972: Summary and Legislative History*, March 1973, https://www.ssa.gov/history/1972amend.html.

100 Ginny McPartland, *Researchers Strive for Decades to Solve Mysteries of Total Health*, May 6, 2012, http://kaiserpermanentehistory.org/tag/chronic-disease/.

101 Gerald Anderson and James R. Knickman, "Changing The Chronic Care System To Meet People's Needs," *Health Affairs* (2001): 146-160.

102 Kimberly Amadeo, "The Rising Cost of Health Care by Year and Its Causes," *The Balance.com*, June 25, 2019, https://www.the-balance.com/causes-of-rising-healthcare-costs-4064878.

103 Library of Congress, *Congress.gov*, 1982, https://www.congress.gov/bill/97th-congress/house-bill/4961.

104 "Analysis of Medicare Hospital Reimbursement Changes in the Tax Equity and Fiscal Responsibility Act of 1982," *cbo. gov.* Congressional Budget Office, March 1983, https://www. cbo.gov/sites/default/files/cbofiles/ftpdocs/50xx/doc5059/ doc09a.pdf.

105 Kimberly Amadeo, "The Rising Cost of Health Care by Year and Its Causes," *The Balance.com*, June 25, 2019, https://www.the-balance.com/causes-of-rising-healthcare-costs-4064878.

106 Ibid.

107 Fiscal Policy Institute, "Escalating Prescription Drug Costs: The Reality and Options for Reform," Testimony Presented to the New York State AFL-CIO Task Force on Prescription Drugs, 2002.

108 Devon M. Herrick, "Unnecessary Regulations that Increase Prescription Drug Costs," *National Center for Policy Analysis*, March 7, 2013, http://www.ncpa.org/pub/st346.

109 Ameet Sarpatwari, "Why Many Generic Drugs Are Becoming So Expensive," *Harvard Health Blog*, October 15, 2015, https://www.health.harvard.edu/blog/why-many-generic-drugs-are-becoming-so-expensive-201510228480.

110 Ibid.

111 KSR Publishing, "U.S. Hospitals Wrestle with Shortages of Drug Supplies Made in Puerto Rico," *Healthcarepurchasing News.com*, October 2017, https://www.hpnonline.com/u.s.hospitals-wrestle-shortages-drug-supplies-made-puerto-rico/.

112 United States Government, "H.R.1 - Medicare Prescription Drug, Improvement, and Modernization Act of 2003," *Congress.Gov*, December 12, 2003, https://www.congress.gov/bill/108th-congress/house-bill/1.

113 "Patient Protection and Affordable Care Act," *Wikipedia: The*

Free Encyclopedia, September 12, 2019, https://en.wikipedia. org/wiki/Patient_Protection_and_Affordable_Care_Act.

114 United States Government, "H.R.1 - Medicare Prescription Drug, Improvement, and Modernization Act of 2003," *Congress.Gov*, December 12, 2003, https://www.congress.gov/ bill/108th-congress/house-bill/1.

115 Melissa Ganz, "The Medicare Prescription Drug, Improvement, & Modernization Act Of 2003: Are We Playing The Lottery With Healthcare Reform?" *3 Duke Law & Technology Review* (2004): 1-20.

116 Robert Book, "After The ACA, How Much Do Health Insurance Mergers Matter?" *Forbes Media*, March 31, 2016, https://www.forbes.com/sites/theapothecary/2016/03/31/ after-the-aca-how-much-do-health-insurance-mergers-matter/#250a2e2d31d8.

117 Ken McDonnell, "History of Health Insurance Benefits," *EmployeeBenefitsResearchInstitute.org*, March 2002, https:// www.ebri.org/publications/facts/index.cfm?fa=0302fact.

118 Mary Gerisch, "Health Care As a Human Right," *Human Rights Magazine* 43, no. 3 (August 1, 2018).

119 Social Security Administration, "Life Expectancy for Social Security," *Social Security History*, n.d., https://www.ssa.gov/ history/lifeexpect.html.

120 Lisa Fayed, "How Much Does the HPV Vaccine Cost?" *VeryWellHealth.com*, April 27, 2017, https://www.verywell.com/ how-much-does-the-hpv-vaccine-cost-514124.

121 National Center for Health Statistics, *Health, United States, 2015: With Special Feature On Racial and Ethnic Health Disparities* (Hyattsville, Maryland: United States Government Printing Office, 2016).

122 U.S. Office of Personnel Management, *Retirement*

Statistics, 2017, https://www.opm.gov/retirement-services/retirement-statistics/.

123 Jeanne Pinder, "Saving Money: Paying Cash for Health Care Even if You're Insured," *ClearHealthCosts.com*, September 4, 2014, http://clearhealthcosts.com/blog/2014/09/saving-money-paying-cash-even-youre-insured-draft/.

124 Gary Wolfram, *Making College More Expensive The Unintended Consequences of Federal Tuition Aid* (Washington D.C.: Cato Institute, 2005).

125 Chris Elkins, "How Much Cancer Costs," *drugwatch.com*, October 7, 2015. https://www.drugwatch.com/2015/10/07/cost-of-cancer/.

126 Dylan Scott, "The Untold Story of TV's First Prescription Drug Ad," *STAT News*, December 5, 2015, https://www.statnews.com/2015/12/11/untold-story-tvs-first-prescription-drug-ad/.

127 PEW Research, "PEW Research Center Religion & Public Life," *Views on End-of-Life Medical Treatments*, November 21, 2013, http://www.pewforum.org/2013/11/21/views-on-end-of-life-medical-treatments/.

128 Christopher P. Adams, and Van V. Brantner, "Estimating The Cost Of New Drug Development: Is It Really $802 Million?" *Health Affairs*, 3 (2006): 420-428.

129 Lacie Glover, "Oncologists Worry About Rising Costs of Cancer Treatment," *U.S. News and World Report*, July 1, 2015, https://health.usnews.com/health-news/patient-advice/articles/2015/07/01/oncologists-worry-about-rising-costs-of-cancer-treatment.

130 Steven Constantino, Nancy J. Hogue, Jennifer Egelhof, and Carrie Germaine, "Program Report: Pharmacy Best Practices and Cost Control Program SFY 2015," *www.leg.state.vt.us/jfo/healthcare*, October 2015, http://www.leg.state.vt.us/jfo/

healthcare/Health%20Reform%20Oversight%20Committee/2015_11_13/Pharmacy%20Best%20Practices%20and%20Cost%20Control%20Report.pdf.

131 RH, anonymous, interview with the author, September 21, 2017.

132 MRI Assist, *MRI Assist*, 2013, http://www.mri-assist.com/.

133 United States Government, "H.R.3590 - Patient Protection and Affordable Care Act," *Congress.Gov*, 2010, https://www.congress.gov/bill/111th-congress/house-bill/3590.

134 Robert Farley, "ACA Impact on Per Capita Cost of Health Care," *FactCheck.org*, February 14, 2014, https://www.factcheck.org/2014/02/aca-impact-on-per-capita-cost-of-health-care/.

135 Christopher Chantrill, *usgovernmentspending.com*. March 29, 2017, http://www.usgovernmentspending.com/total_spending.

136 Abby Goodnough and Robert Pear, "Unable to Meet the Deductible or the Doctor," *New York Times*, October 24, 2014, https://www.nytimes.com/2014/10/18/us/unable-to-meet-the-deductible-or-the-doctor.html.

137 Jeffery Young, "AMA Endorses Senate Healthcare Reform Bill," *TheHill.com*, December 29, 2009, http://thehill.com/homenews/senate/73249-ama-endorses-senate-health-bill.

138 Christine Eibner, Peter S. Hussey, Federico Girosi, "The Effects of the Affordable Care Act on Workers' Health Insurance Coverage," *New England Journal of Medicine* (2010): 1393-1395.

139 Susanne Madden, "Participating in New Healthcare Exchange Plans," *PhysiciansPractice.com*, February 19, 2014, http://www.physicianspractice.com/healthcare-reform/participating-new-healthcare-exchange-plans.

140 Zachary Tracer and Katherine Greifeld, "Aetna CEO: Obamacare in "Death Spiral," *Bloomberg Business*, February 15, 2017, https://www.bloomberg.com/news/articles/2017-02-15/aetna-ceo-says-obamacare-in-a-death-spiral-with-sick-customers.

141 Stephen Parente, "Affordable Care Act Will Deliver a Big Surprise in 2017," *Pennlive.com.*, December 15, 2014, http://www.pennlive.com/opinion/2014/12/affordable_care_act_obamacare_1.html?ath=ff683cc159rb3e2bae51d60b23238e7c.

142 "3 Things to Know before You Pick a Health Insurance Plan," *Healthcare.gov*, Department of Health and Human Services, 2017, https://www.healthcare.gov/choose-a-plan/comparing-plans/.

143 Xtelligent Healthcare Media, LLC, *How the Affordable Care Act Changed the Face of Health Insurance*, June 15, 2016, https://healthpayerintelligence.com/features/how-the-affordable-care-act-changed-the-face-of-health-insurance.

144 Gary Claxton, et al., "Health Benefits In 2013: Moderate Premium Increases In Employer-Sponsored Plans," *Health Affairs* (2013): 1667-1676.

145 Paul Ketchel, "Patient Guide: High-Deductible Health Care Plans." *nydailyviews.com*, March 11, 2016, http://www.nydailynews.com/life-style/patient-guide-high-deductible-health-care-plans-article-1.2561857.

146 John C. Goodman, "Are High Deductibles A Good Thing? Part 1," *Forbes.com*, March 7, 2016, https://www.forbes.com/sites/johngoodman/2016/03/07/are-high-deductibles-a-good-thing-part-i/#5e263d947290.

147 KK, anonymous, interview with the author, February 2018.

148 Brooke Murphy, "21 Statistics on High-Deductible Health Plans," *Beckershospitalreview.com*, May 19, 2016, http://www.beckershospitalreview.com/

finance/21-statistics-on-high-deductible-health-plans.
html.

149 "The Affordable Care Act and Its Effect on Your Tax Refund,"
Refundschedule.com. December 2, 2014, https://www.refund-
schedule.com/affordable-care-act-tax-refund/.

150 "What Are the Average Physician Overhead Rates
in 2017?" *LiveClinic Healthcare Blog*, February 16,
2017, http://liveclinic.com/blog/practice-management/
physician-overheard-rates-2017/.

151 PF, anonymous, interview the author, October 2017.

152 Tara O'Neill Hayes, "Are Electronic Medical Records Worth the
Costs of Implementation?" *American Action Forum*, August
6, 2015, https://www.americanactionforum.org/research/
are-electronic-medical-records-worth-the-costs-of-imple-
mentation/.

153 Chad D. Meyerhoefer, et al., "The Consequences of Electronic
Health Record Adoption for Physician Productivity and Birth
Outcomes," *ILR Review* (2016): 860-869.

154 Douglas O. Staigner, David I. Auerbach, and Peter I. Buerhaus, "Trends in the Work Hours of Physicians in the United
States," *Journal of American Medical Association* (2010):
747-753.

155 Jeff Gitlen, "Average Medical School Debt," *lendeu.
com*, February 15, 2017, https://lendedu.com/blog/
average-medical-school-debt/.

156 American Medical News. *http://www.amednews.com/arti-
cle/20120827/profession/308279940/6/.* August 27, 2012.

157 Nina Lincoff, "The Future of Healthcare Could Be in Concierge Medicine," *Healthline*, June 30, 2015, https://www.
healthline.com/health-news/the-future-of-healthcare-could-
be-in-concierge-medicine-063015#1.

158 Aaron Young, Humayun J. Chaudhry, Xiaomei Pei, Katie Arnhart, Michael Dugan, and Scott A. Steingard, "A Census of Actively Licensed Physicians in the United States, 2016," *Journal of Medical Regulation* (2017): 7-21.

159 KKF's State Health Facts, *Professionally Active Physicians*, March 2019, https://www.kff.org/other/state-indicator/total-active-physicians/?currentTimeframe=0&sortModel=%7B%22colId%22:%22Location%22,%22sort%22:%22asc%22%7D.

160 Suneel Dhand, "Pareto's Principle in Hospital Medicine," *DocTHinx*, December 2, 2014, http://suneeldhand.com/2014/12/02/paretos-principle-in-hospital-medicine/.

161 Jeffery Parks, "How Algorithm Driven Medicine Can Affect Patient Care," *KevinMD.com*, January 30, 2012, https://www.kevinmd.com/blog/2012/01/algorithm-driven-medicine-affect-patient-care.html.

162 Jennifer Perry, Foster Mobley, and Matt Brubaker, "Most Doctors Have Little or No Management Training, and That's a Problem," *Harvard Business Review*, December 15, 2017, https://hbr.org/2017/12/most-doctors-have-little-or-no-management-training-and-thats-a-problem.

163 Enrico Portuese and Trevor Orchard, *Mortality in Insulin-Dependent Diabetes* (Bethesda, Marylannd: NIH, 1995).

164 Centers for Disease Control and Prevention, *Working to Reverse the US Epidemic*, July 25, 2016, https://www.cdc.gov/chronicdisease/resources/publications/aag/diabetes.htm.

165 Ford, ES, Ajani, UA, et al. "Explaining the Decrease in U. S. Deaths from Coronary Disease, 1980-2000." *New England Journal of Medicine*, 2007: 2388.

166 Alexandra N. Nowbar, Mauro Gitto, James, P. Howard, Darrel P. Francis, and Rasha Al-Lamee, "Mortality From Ischemic

Heart Disease," *Circulation: Cardiovascular Quality and Outcomes* (June 2019): 1-11.

167 Kathi E. Hanna, Editor, *Biomedical Politics* (Washington, D. C.: National Academy Press, 1991).

168 National Institute of Health, *Kidney Disease Statistics for the United States*, December 2016, https://www.niddk.nih.gov/health-information/health-statistics/kidney-disease.

169 Jeffrey M. Jones, "Americans Seeing Doctors More Often," *Gallup.com*, November 30, 2004, http://www.gallup.com/poll/14194/Americans-Seeing-Doctors-More-Often.aspx.

170 "Number of Doctor Visits per Capita in Selected Countries as of 2015," *Statista.com*, 2017, https://www.statista.com/statistics/236589/number-of-doctor-visits-per-capita-by-country/.

171 American Heart Association, "Heart Failure Patients Have More Doctor Visits, Medications Than Others On Medicare," *ScienceDaily.com*, November 2008.

172 Donald J. Trump, "Executive Order on Advancing American Kidney Health," *Whitehouse.gov*, July 10, 2019, https://www.whitehouse.gov/presidential-actions/executive-order-advancing-american-kidney-health/.

173 Judy A. Bielby, "Evolution of DRGs (2010 update)," *AHIMA.org*, April 2010, http://library.ahima.org/doc?oid=106590#.WRkOL4WcGUk.

174 "A 'Nightmare' for Surgeons? Medicare Is Ending Global Payments for Surgeries," Advisory Board, November 13, 2014, https://www.advisory.com/daily-briefing/2014/11/13/a-nightmare-for-surgeons-medicare-is-ending-global-payments-for-surgeries.

175 National Council on Disability, "Appendix B. A Brief History

of Managed Care," *NCD.gov*, 2013, http://www.ncd.gov/publications/2013/20130315/20130513_AppendixB.

176 Ibid.

177 Lyle Nelson, *Lessons from Medicare's Demonstration Projects on Value-Based Payment* (Washington, D.C.: Congressional Budget Office, 2012).

178 Leo Issac, "Online Learning for Sports Management," *LeoIssac.com*, 2013, http://www.leoisaac.com/budget/bud031.htm.

179 UnitedStatesRenalDataSystem, "Costs of ESRD," *usrds.org*, 2013, https://www.usrds.org/2013/view/v2_11.aspx.

180 Anne Pfuntner, Lauren M. Wier, and Claudia Steiner, *Costs for Hospital Stays in the United States, 2011*, HCUP Statistical Brief #168, (Rockville, MD: Agency for Healthcare Research and Quality, 2013).

181 Congress.gov, *H.R.1 - American Recovery and Reinvestment Act of 2009*, https://www.congress.gov/bill/111th-congress/house-bill/1/text.

182 U.S. Department of Health and Human Services Food and Drug Administration, *Use of Electronic Health Record Data in Clinical Investigations*, Procedural Guideline, (Washington, D.C.: United States Government, 2018).

183 H.M. Wee and Simon Wu, "Lean Supply Chain: Learning from the Toyota Production System," *Emerald Group Publishing Group Limited*, 2009, file:///E:/Patient%20Based%20Medical%20Care/toyota_tps2015.pdf.

184 RH, anonymous, interview with the author, September 21, 2017.

185 Dennis C. Crawford, Chuan Silvia LI, Sheila Sprague, and Mohit Bhandari, "Clinical and Cost Implications of Inpatient Versus Outpatient Orthopedic Surgeries: A Systematic

Review of the Published Literature," *Orthopedic Reviews* (2015): 116-121.

186 Sable-Smith Bram, "Insulin's High Cost Leads To Lethal Rationing," *Shots Health News from NPR*, September 1, 2018, https://www.npr.org/sections/health-shots/2018/09/01/641615877/insulins-high-cost-leads-to-lethal-rationing.

187 Tobias Dreischulte, et al., "Safer Prescribing — A Trial of Education, Informatics, and Financial Incentives," *New England Journal of Medicine* (2016): 1053-1064.

188 MD Toolbox, *E-Prescribing Mandate State Laws*, 2019, https://www.mdtoolbox.com/(X(1)S(yiuqjnn2xghzo0vj4w3dtxvf))/eprescribe-map.aspx.

189 Brendan Murphy, "For First Time, Physician Practice Owners Are Not the Majority," *AMA-assn.org economics*, American Medical Association, May 31, 2017, https://www.ama-assn.org/practice-management/economics/first-time-physician-practice-owners-are-not-majority.

190 Lawrence Casalino, et al., "Large Independent Primary Care Medical Groups," *Annals of Family Medicine* (2016): 16-25.

191 John Maxfield, "A Timeline of Wells Fargo's Sales Scandal," *The Motley Fool*, September 24, 2017, https://www.fool.com/investing/2017/09/24/a-timeline-of-wells-fargos-sales-scandal.aspx.

192 John Maxfield, "A Timeline of Wells Fargo's Sales Scandal," *The Motley Fool*, September 24, 2017, https://www.fool.com/investing/2017/09/24/a-timeline-of-wells-fargos-sales-scandal.aspx.

193 U. S. Department of Health and Human Services, "Duty Hours and Patient Safety," *Agency for Healthcare Research*

and Quality, August 2018, https://psnet.ahrq.gov/primers/primer/19.

194 Ibid.

195 David Orentlicher, "Controlling Health Care Spending: More Patient 'Skin in the Game?'" *Indiana Health Law Review* (2016): 348-362.

196 Robin Cohen and Emily Zammitti, *High-deductible Health Plans and Financial Barriers to Medical Care: Early Release of Estimates From the National Health Interview Survey, 2016*, National Health Interview Survey Early Release Program, (Washington, D.C.: U.S. Department of Health and Human Services, June 2017).

197 Bryan R. Haynes, et al., "Management of Patient Compliance in the Treatment of Hypertension," *Hypertension* (1982): 415-423.

198 Samuel Y. S. Wong and Albert Lee, "Communication Skills and Doctor Patient Relationship," *The Hong Kong Medical Diary* (March 2006): 7-9.

199 Vivify Health, *Turning Patients into Engaged Customers*, 2017, https://www.vivifyhealth.com/patients-to-customers/.

200 Kristin Carman, et al., "Patient And Family Engagement: A Framework For Understanding The Elements And Developing Interventions And Policies," *Health Affairs Journal* (February 2013): 223-231.

201 Lucas M. Bachmann, Florian S. Gutzwiller, Milo A. Puhan, Johann Steurer, Claudia Steurer-Stey, and Gerd Gigerenzer, "Do citizens have minimum medical knowledge? A survey," *BioMedCentral Medicine* (2007): 1-6.

202 Oneil Williams, "Micromanagement's Effect on Productivity," *AZcentral.com*, 2018, https://yourbusiness.azcentral.com/micromanagements-effect-productivity-14238.html.

203 Jersey Chen, Saif S. Rathore, Yongfei Wang, Martha J. Radford, and Harlan M. Krumholz, "Physician Board Certification and the Care and Outcomes of Elderly Patients with Acute Myocardial Infarction," *Journal of General Internal Medicine* (2006): 238–244.

204 Robert Anthony, *UBM Medica*, 2010, https://www.roswellpark. org/partners-practice/white-papers/board-certification.

205 Stephanie Tulia, "Executive Coaching and the American President," *AdvancingWomen.com*, 2005, http://advancing-women.com/coaching/executive_coaching_and_the_american_president.php.

206 Richard D. White, "The Micromanagement Disease: Symptoms, Diagnosis, and Cure," *Public Personnel Management* (2010): 71-76.

207 Ibid.

208 David B. Reuben and Mary E. Tinetti, "Goal-Oriented Patient Care — An Alternative Health Outcomes Paradigm," *New England Journal of Medicine* (March 1, 2012): 777-779.

209 James Beck, "Boards Micromanging," *EffectiveGovernance. com*, August 22, 2016, https://www.effectivegovernance.com. au/boards-micromanaging/.

210 Michael Schuyler, *Why the U.S. Postal Service Is in Greater Financial Trouble than Most Foreign Postal Services - The Role of Governement Micromanagement*, Congressional Advisory No. 282, (Washington, D.C.: Institute for Research on the Economics of Taxation, 2012).

211 John Henning Shumann, "A Bygone Era: When Bipartisanship Led To Health Care Transformation," *National Public Radio*, October 2, 2016, https://www.npr.org/sections/health-shots/2016/10/02/495775518/a-bygone-era-when-bipartisanship-led-to-health-care-transformation.

212 Greg Bordonaro, "Hospitals Using Debt for Growth," *Hartford Business Journal*, November 12, 2012, https://www.hartford-business.com/article/hospitals-using-debt-for-growth.

213 Jean Murray, "What is a Section 179 Deduction?" *The Balance Small Business*, January 5, 2020, https://www.thebalancesmb.com/what-is-a-section-179-deduction-397650.

214 Jean Murray, "Bonus Depreciation and How It Affects Business Taxes," *The Balance Small Business*, August 11, 2019, https://www.thebalancesmb.com/what-is-bonus-depreciation-398144.

215 Bob Heman, "10 Statistics on Hospital Labor Costs as a Percentage of Operating Revenue," *BeckersHospitalReview.com*, December 10, 2013, http://www.beckershospitalreview.com/finance/10-statistics-on-hospital-labor-costs-as-a-percentage-of-operating-revenue.html.

216 American College of Physicians, *American College of Physicians Policy on Provider-Based Billing*, April 2013, https://www.acponline.org/acp_policy/policies/provider_based_billing_2013.pdf.

217 Smith and Howard, Certified Public Accounts and Advisors. *2018 Tax Cuts & Jobs Act Overview*, March 2018, https://www.smith-howard.com/2018-tax-cuts-jobs-act-overview/.

218 Leslie Greenwald, et al., "Specialty Versus Community Hospitals: Referrals, Quality, And Community Benefits," *Health Affairs* (2006): 106-118.

219 Management Sciences for Health, *Evaluating the Cost of Pharmaceuticals*, training course participant guide (Arlington, Virginia: U.S. Agency for International Development by the Rational Pharmaceutical Management Plus Program, 2007).

220 David Belk and Paul Belk, "The Pharmaceutical Industry,"

Truecostofhealthcare.org, 2018, http://truecostofhealthcare.org/the_pharmaceutical_industry/.

221 Ibid.

222 Campaign for Sustainable Rx Pricing, *The Facts about Rising Prescription Drug Costs*, 2016, http://www.csrxp.org/wp-content/uploads/2016/04/CSRxP_Facts-of-Rising-Rx-Prices.pdf.

223 United States Government Accountability Office, *GAO-16-706 Generic Drugs under Medicare*, Report to Congressional Requesters (Washington, D.C.: United States Government, 2016).

224 *"Unapproved Drugs Initiative," Wikipedia, The Free Encyclopedia*, April 1, 2016, https://en.wikipedia.org/wiki/Unapproved_Drugs_Initiative.

225 Michael R. Law, Lucy Cheng, Irfan A. Dhalla, Deborah Heard, and Steven G. Morgan, "The Effect of Cost on Adherence to Prescription Medications in Canada," *Canadian Medical Association Journal* (February 21, 2012): 297-302.

226 Candice Malcolm, "The Pitfalls of Single-Payer Health Care: Canada's Cautionary Tale," *National Review*, April 13, 2017, https://www.nationalreview.com/2017/04/canada-single-payer-health-care-system-failures-cautionary-tale/.

227 Ana Mulero, "Gottlieb Offers Solutions for High Generic Drug Prices, Real-Time Postmarket Surveillance," *Regulatory Affairs Professionals Society*, April 25, 2018, https://www.raps.org/news-and-articles/news-articles/2018/4/gottlieb-offers-solutions-for-high-generic-drug-pr.

228 World Health Organization, *Essential Medicines and Health Products Information Portal*, December 6, 2017, http://apps.who.int/medicinedocs/en/d/Js4907e/3.8.html.

229 Cristina Arnes and Guilherme Cintra, *The Pharmaceutical*

Industry and Global Health: Facts and Figures 2017, Industry Report (Geneva, Switzerland: International Federation of Pharmaceutical Manufacturers & Associations, 2017).

230 Christopher VanLang, "How Much of New Drug Research Is Funded by the Government Compared to Charities as Well as Pharmaceutical Companies Themselves?" *Quora.com*, October 21, 2016, https://www.quora.com/How-much-of-new-drug-research-is-funded-by-the-government-compared-to-charities-as-well-as-pharmaceutical-companies-themselves.

231 Thomas A. Abbott and John A. Vernon, *The Cost of US Pharmaceutical Price Reductions: A Financial Simulation Model of R&D Decisions*, 2004-2005 Finance Department Seminar Series at the University of Connecticut (Cambridge, MA: National Bureau of Economic Research, 2005).

232 John C. Goodman, "Are High Deductibles A Good Thing? Part 1," *Forbes.com*, March 7, 2016, https://www.forbes.com/sites/johngoodman/2016/03/07/are-high-deductibles-a-good-thing-part-i/#5e263d947290.

233 Kwanghui Lim, "The Relationship between Research and Innovation in the Semiconductor and Pharmaceutical Industries (1981–1997)," *Research Policy* (2004): 287–321.

234 Chris Isidore, Tal Kopan, and Julia Horowitz, "Closed Puerto Rico Factories Are the Sole Source of Some Critical Drugs," *CNN Money*, September 29, 2017, https://money.cnn.com/2017/09/29/news/companies/puerto-rico-drug-makers/index.html.

235 Food and Drug Administration, "Current Good Manufacturing Practice for Finished Pharmaceuticals," *Code of Regulations Title 21 Volume 4*, (Washington, D.C.: United States Food and Drug Administration, April 1, 2018).

236 Sachin Jain, *What are the Main Purposes of*

Advertising?, n.d., http://www.shareyouressays.com/essays/what-are-the-main-purposes-of-advertising/89394.

237 David Belk and Paul Belk, "The Pharmaceutical Industry," *Truecostofhealthcare.org*, 2018, http://truecostofhealthcare.org/the_pharmaceutical_industry/.

238 Andrea Hardaway, *The Top 6 Reasons Process Improvement Initiatives Fail*, July 21, 2015, https://www.linkedin.com/pulse/top-6-reasons-process-improvement-operational-fail-andrea.

239 United States Congress, "H.R. 3128 (99th): Consolidated Omnibus Budget Reconciliation Act of 1985," *Govtrack.us*, April 7, 1986, https://www.govtrack.us/congress/bills/99/hr3128/text.

240 —. "H.R.5835 - Omnibus Budget Reconciliation Act of 1990," *Congress.gov*, November 5, 1990, https://www.congress.gov/bill/101st-congress/house-bill/5835/text.

241 —. "Health Insurance Portability and Accountability Act of 1996," *Congressional Record: 142* (August 21, 1996): 1935-2103.

242 United States Government, "H.R.1 - Medicare Prescription Drug, Improvement, and Modernization Act of 2003," *Congress.gov*, December 12, 2003, https://www.congress.gov/bill/108th-congress/house-bill/1.

243 Hinda Chaikind, "P.L. 110-275: The Medicare Improvements for Patients and Providers Act of 2008," *Congressional Research Service*, July 23, 2008, file:///D:/Documents/My%20Documents/Patient%20Based%20Medical%20Care/MIPPA%20act%20of%202008.pdf.

244 United States Congress, "H.R.1 - American Recovery and Reinvestment Act of 2009," *Congress.gov*, February 17, 2009, https://www.congress.gov/bill/111th-congress/house-bill/1/text.

245 —. "H.R.3590 - Patient Protection and Affordable Care Act," *Congress.gov*, 2010, https://www.congress.gov/bill/111th-congress/house-bill/3590.

246 —. "Food and Drug Administration Safety and Innovation Act," *Congressional Record: 158* (July 9, 2012): 993-1132.

247 —. "H.R.2 - Medicare Access and CHIP Reauthorization Act of 2015," *Congress.gov*, 2015, https://www.congress.gov/bill/114th-congress/house-bill/2.

248 —. "21st Century Cures Act," *Congressional Record: 162* (December 13, 2016): 1033-1344.

249 —. "Public Law 115–97—December 22, 2017," *Congressional Record: 163* (December 22, 2017): 2092.

250 Wellness Directory of Minnesota, "The Nature of the Pharmaceutical Industry," *mnwelldir.org*, n.d., http://www.mnwelldir.org/docs/editorial/pharm.htm.

251 Klaus M. Leisinger, "Meeting the Global Health Challenge: The Role of the Pharmaceutical Industry," *Makingitmagazine.com*, October 31, 2012, http://www.makingitmagazine.net/?p=6046.

251 United States Congress, "Act of July 2, 1890 (Sherman Anti-Trust Act)," *Enrolled Acts and Resolutinos of Congress, 1789-1992; General Records of the United States Government, Record Group 11* (Washington, D.C.: National Archives, July 2, 1890).

252—. "An Act to Supplement Existing Laws Against Unlawful Restraints," *govtrackus.s3.amazonaws.com*, 1914, https://govtrackus.s3.amazonaws.com/legislink/pdf/stat/38/STATUTE-38-Pg730.pdf.

253 United States Government, "H.R.1 - Medicare Prescription Drug, Improvement, and Modernization Act of 2003," *Congress.gov*, December 12, 2003, https://www.congress.gov/bill/108th-congress/house-bill/1.

254 Olen Bruce, "How Can the Government Influence the Allocation of Resources in a Country?" *eNotes Editorial*, March 19, 2013, https://www.enotes.com/homework-help/how-government-could-influence-allocation-422406.

255 New York State Task Force on Life and the Law and New York State Department of Health, *Ventilator Allocation Guidelines*, Task Force Report (Albany: State of New York, 2015).

256 Audrey McNamara, "Cuomo Warns New York Is 'Still on the Way up the Mountain' as Virus Cases Top 30,000," *CBS News*, March 25, 2020, https://www.cbsnews.com/news/new-york-cuomo-cases-over-30000/.

257 Norman Fost, "Who Should Get the Last Ventilator?" *Future-Tense*, April 3, 2020, https://slate.com/technology/2020/04/coronavirus-ventilator-ethical-guidelines.html.

258 Nick Romeo, "The Grim Ethical Dilemma of Rationing Medical Care, Explained," *Vox.com*, March 31, 2020, https://www.vox.com/coronavirus-covid19/2020/3/31/21199721/coronavirus-covid-19-hospitals-triage-rationing-italy-new-york.

259 New York Department of Health, "Advisory: Hospital Discharges and Admissions to Nursing Homes," (Albany: State of New York, March 25, 2020).

260 Associated Press, "U.S. COVID-19 Deaths Top 1,000," *www.jems.com*, March 26, 2020, https://www.jems.com/2020/03/26/u-s-covid-19-deaths-top-1000/.

261 Joe Mahoney, "New York Faces Growing Wave of COVID-19 Deaths at Nursing Homes," *The Daily Star* (Oneonta, NY), April 22, 2020.

262 Karen Weise, Amy Fink, and Sheri Harmon, "Why Washington State? How Did It Start? Questions Answered on the U.S. Coronavirus Outbreak," *New York Times*, March 4, 2020, https://www.nytimes.com/2020/03/04/us/coronavirus-in-washington-state.html.

263 "2020 Coronavirus Pandemic in New York (State)," *Wikipedia, The Free Encyclopedia*, May 1, 2020, https://en.wikipedia.org/w/index.php?title=2020_coronavirus_pandemic_in_New_York_(state)&oldid=954327925.

264 Steve Forbes, "The Horrid Economic Consequences of World War I -- We Still Suffer From Them," *Forbes Media*, August 14, 2014, https://www.forbes.com/sites/steveforbes/2014/08/02/economic-consequences-of-the-great-war/#7eac6c6d2b21.

265 American Hospital Association, *Regulatory Overload: Assessing the Regulatory Burden on Health Systems, Hospitals and Post-acute Care Providers*, Members Report (Washington, D.C.: American Hospital Association, 2017).

Bibliography

"2020 Coronavirus Pandemic in New York (State)," *Wikipedia, The Free Encyclopedia*, May 1, 2020, https://en.wikipedia.org/w/index.php?title=2020_coronavirus_pandemic_in_New_York_(state)&oldid=954327925.

Abbott, Thomas A., and John A. Vernon. *The Cost of US Pharmaceutical Price Reductions: A Financial Simulation Model of R&D Decisions.* 2004-2005 Finance Department Seminar Series at the University of Connecticut, Cambridge, MA: National Bureau of Economic Research, 2005.

Accreditation Council for Graduate Medical Education. *Common Program Requirements.* Chicago, IL, September 26, 2010.

Adams, Christopher P. and Brantner, Van V. "Estimating The Cost Of New Drug Development: Is It Really $802 Million?" *Health Affairs* (March 2006): 420-428.

"Affordable Care Act and It's Effect on Your Tax Refund, The." *Refundschedule.com.* December 2, 2014. https://www.refund-schedule.com/affordable-care-act-tax-refund/.

Alguire, Patrick C. "Understanding Capitation." *American College of Physicians.* January 27, 2018. https://www.acponline.org/about-acp/about-internal-medicine/career-paths/residency-career-counseling/guidance/understanding-capitation.

Amadeo, Kimberly. "The Rising Cost of Health Care by Year and

Its Causes." *The Balance.com.* June 25, 2019. https://www.the-balance.com/causes-of-rising-healthcare-costs-4064878.

American College of Physicians. *American College of Physicians Policy on Provider-Based Billing.* April 2013. https://www.acp-online.org/acp_policy/policies/provider_based_billing_2013.pdf.

American Hospital Association. *Regulatory Overload: Assessing the Regulatory Burden on Health Systems, Hospitals and Post-acute Care Providers.* Members Report, Washington, D.C.: American Hospital Association, 2017.

American Lithotripsy Soc. v. Thompson, 215 F. Supp. 2d 23 (D.D.C. 2002). 1:01-cv-1812 (District Court, District of Columbia, July 12, 2002).

American Medical Association. *Billing Medicaid Patients.* 1999. http://www.whatismedicalinsurancebilling.org/2009/10/billing-medicaid-patients.html.

American Medical News. *http://www.amednews.com/article/20120827/profession/308279940/6/.* August 27, 2012.

Anderson, Gerald and Knickman, James R. "Changing The Chronic Care System To Meet People's Needs." *Health Affairs* (2001): 146-160.

Anthony, Robert. *UBM Medica.* 2010. https://www.roswellpark.org/partners-practice/white-papers/board-certification.

Arnes, Cristina and Guilherme Cintra. *The Pharmaceutical Industry and Global Health: Facts and Figures 2017.* Industry Report, Geneva, Switzerland: International Federation of Pharmaceutical Manufacturers & Associations, 2017.

Ashbaugh, John and Gary Smith. "Capitation and Risk Management." *Human Services Research Institute.* January 6, 1996. https://view.officeapps.live.com/op/view.aspx?src=https%3A%2F%2Fwww.hsri.

org%2Ffiles%2Fuploads%2Fpublications%2FMC103Capita-tionandRiskManagement.DOC.

Associated Press. "U.S. COVID-19 Deaths Top 1,000." *www.jems.com*. March 26, 2020. https://www.jems.com/2020/03/26/u-s-covid-19-deaths-top-1000/.

Bachmann, Lucas M., Florian S. Gutzwiller, Milo A. Puhan, Johann Steurer, Claudia Steurer-Stey, and Gerd Gigerenzer. "Do citizens have minimum medical knowledge? A survey." *BioMedCentral Medicine* (2007): 1-6.

Baily, Brianna. "Help Wanted: Oklahoma Faces Shortage of Healthcare Workers." *NewsOk.com*. 2015. http://newsok.com/article/5452886.

Baker, Robert. "The Eighteenth-Century." In *The Codification of Medical Morality*, edited by Robert Baker, Dorothy Porter, and Roy Porter, 93-98. Kluwer Academic Publishers, 1993.

Ball, Robert M. *Social Security Amendments of 1972: Summary and Legislative History*. March 1973. https://www.ssa.gov/history/1972amend.html.

Beck, James. "Boards Micromanging." *EffectiveGovernance.com*. August 22, 2016. https://www.effectivegovernance.com.au/boards-micromanaging/.

Belk, David and Paul Belk. "The Pharmaceutical Industry." *Truecostofhealthcare.org*. 2018. http://truecostofhealthcare.org/the_pharmaceutical_industry/.

Bielby, Judy A. "Evolution of DRGs (2010 Update)." *AHIMA.org*. April 2010. http://library.ahima.org/doc?oid=106590#.WRkOL4WcGUk.

Bisera, Cheryl. "How High Deductibles Impact Patients, Practices." *DermatologyTimes*. October 17, 2014. http://dermatologytimes.modernmedicine.com/dermatology-times/news/how-high-de-ductibles-impact-patients-practices?page=full.

Blake, Valerie. "When Is a Patient-Physician Relationship Established?" *AMA Journal of Ethics* (2012): 403-406.

Blue Cross Blue Shield. *An Industry Pioneer: Leading the Way in Health Insurance.* 2019. https://www.bcbs.com/about-us/industry-pioneer.

Book, Robert. "After The ACA, How Much Do Health Insurance Mergers Matter?" *Forbes Media.* March 31, 2016. https://www.forbes.com/sites/theapothecary/2016/03/31/after-the-aca-how-much-do-health-insurance-mergers-matter/#250a2e2d31d8.

Bordonaro, Greg. "Hospitals using debt for growth." *Hartford Business Journal.* November 12, 2012. https://www.hartford-business.com/article/hospitals-using-debt-for-growth.

Bram, Sable-Smith. "Insulin's High Cost Leads To Lethal Rationing." *Shots Health News from NPR.* September 1, 2018. https://www.npr.org/sections/health-shots/2018/09/01/641615877/insulins-high-cost-leads-to-lethal-rationing.

Bruce, Olen. "How Can the Government Influence the Allocation of Resources in a Country?" *eNotes Editorial.* March 19, 2013. https://www.enotes.com/homework-help/how-government-could-influence-allocation-422406.

Brumley, Sarah. "What Is Quality Assurance in Health Care?" *Chron.com.* 2017. http://smallbusiness.chron.com/quality--assurance-health-care-76135.html.

Buff, Maureen and Terrell, Timothy J. "The Role of Third Party Payers in Medical Cost Increases." *Journal of American Physicians and Surgeons* (2014): 75-79.

Campaign for Sustainable Rx Pricing. *The Facts about Rising Prescription Drug Costs.* 2016. http://www.csrxp.org/wp-content/uploads/2016/04/CSRxP_Facts-of-Rising-Rx-Prices.pdf.

Carman, Kristin L., et al. "Patient And Family Engagement: A

Framework For Understanding The Elements And Developing Interventions And Policies." *Health Affairs* (February 2013): 223-231.

Casalino, Lawrence P., et al. "Large Independent Primary Care Medical Groups." *Annals of Family Medicine* (2016): 16-25.

Center for Disease Control and Prevention. "State HIV Testing Laws: Consent and Counseling Requirements." *CDC.gov.* March 15, 2015. https://www.cdc.gov/hiv/policies/law/states/testing.html.

Center for Medicare and Medicaid Services. *ESRD Conditions for Coverage (CfCs) Final Rule Rollout.* August 28, 2008. file:///D:/My%20Documents/Patient%20Based%20Medical%20Care/FAQsESRDRolloutFINAL082808.pdf.

Centers for Disease Control and Prevention. *Working to Reverse the US Epidemic.* July 25, 2016. https://www.cdc.gov/chronic-disease/resources/publications/aag/diabetes.htm.

Chaikind, Hinda. "P.L. 110-275: The Medicare Improvements for Patients and Providers Act of 2008." *Congressional Research Service.* July 23, 2008. file:///D:/Documents/My%20Documents/Patient%20Based%20Medical%20Care/MIPPA%20act%20of%202008.pdf.

Chantrill, Christopher. *usgovernmentspending.com.* March 29, 2017. http://www.usgovernmentspending.com/total_spending.

Chen, Jersey, Saif S. Rathore, Yongfei Wang, Martha J. Radford, and Harlan M. Krumholz. "Physician Board Certification and the Care and Outcomes of Elderly Patients with Acute Myocardial Infarction." *Journal of General Internal Medicine* (2006): 238–244.

Claxton, Gary, et al. "Health Benefits In 2013: Moderate Premium Increases In Employer-Sponsored Plans." *Health Affairs* (2013): 1667-1676.

CMA Health Policy Consultants. *The Center for Medicare Advocacy.* 2017. http://www.medicareadvocacy.org/medicare-info/quality-of-care/.

Cohen, Robin A. and Zammitti, Emily P. *High-deductible Health Plans and Financial Barriers to Medical Care: Early Release of Estimates From the National Health Interview Survey, 2016.* National Health Interview Survey Early Release Program, Washington, D.C.: U.S. Department of Health and Human Services, 2017.

Concierge Medicine Today. *Concierge Medicine Today.* May 2017. https://conciergemedicinetoday.org/concierge-medicine-cost/.

Congress.gov. *H.R.1 - American Recovery and Reinvestment Act of 2009.* February 17, 2009. https://www.congress.gov/bill/111th-congress/house-bill/1/text.

Congressional Budget Office. "Analysis of Medicare Hospital Reimbursement Changes in the Tax Equity and Fiscal Responsibility Act of 1982." *Cbo.gov.* March 1983. https://www.cbo.gov/sites/default/files/cbofiles/ftpdocs/50xx/doc5059/doc09a.pdf.

Constantino, Steven, Commissioner, Nancy J., PharmD Hogue, Jennifer, MBA Egelhof, and Carrie, EMT-CPC Germaine. "Program Report: Pharmacy Best Practices and Cost Control Program SFY 2015." *www.leg.state.vt.us/jfo/healthcare.* 10 2015. http://www.leg.state.vt.us/jfo/healthcare/Health%20Reform%20Oversight%20Committee/2015_11_13/Pharmacy%20Best%20Practices%20and%20Cost%20Control%20Report.pdf.

Crawford, Dennis C., Silvia Li Chuan, Sheila Sprague, and Mohit Bhandari. "Clinical and Cost Implications of Inpatient Versus Outpatient Orthopedic Surgeries: A Systematic Review of the Published Literature." *Orthopedic Reviews* (2015): 116-121.

Dhand, Suneel. "Pareto's Principle in Hospital Medicine." *DocTHinx*. December 2, 2014. http://suneeldhand. com/2014/12/02/paretos-principle-in-hospital-medicine/.

Dixon-Fyle, Sundiatu, et al. "Changing Patient Behavior: The Next Frontier in Healthcare Value." *Health International* (2012): 64-73.

ECRI. "ECRI Institute's 21st Annual Conference The 'New' Complex Patient: The Shifting Locus of Care and Cost ." *ECRI. org*. Novemberber 2014. https://www.ecri.org/Resources/Conference/The-New-Complex-Patient-Conference-Summary. pdf.

Eibner, Christine, Peter S. Hussey, and Federico Girosi. "The Effects of the Affordable Care Act on Workers' Health Insurance Coverage." *New England Journal of Medicine* (2010): 1393-1395.

Eichenwald, Kurt. "A Certified Medical Controversy." *Newsweek.com*. April 7, 2015. http://www.newsweek.com/ certified-medical-controversy-320495.

Elkins, Chris. "How Much Cancer Costs." *drugwatch.com*. October 7, 2015. https://www.drugwatch.com/2015/10/07/ cost-of-cancer/.

Epstein, R.M. and Hundert, E. M. "Defining and Assessing Professional Competence." *Journal of the American Medical Association* (2002): 226-235.

Evans, H M. "Do Patients Have Duties?" *Journal of Medical Ethics* (2007): 689-694.

"Every Student Succeeds Act." June 18, 2018. *Wikipedia, The Free Encyclopedia*. June 24, 2018. https://en.wikipedia.org/wiki/ Every_Student_Succeeds_Act.

Fairbanks, Arthur. "Pythagoras and the Pythagoreans Translated

1898." *Hanover Historical Texts Project.* June 2013. https://history. hanover.edu/texts/presoc/pythagor.html.

Farley, Robert. "ACA Impact on Per Capita Cost of Health Care." *Fact-Check.org.* February 14, 2014. https://www.factcheck.org/2014/02/ aca-impact-on-per-capita-cost-of-health-care/.

Fayed, Lisa. "How Much Does the HPV Vaccine Cost?" *Very-WellHealth.com.* April 27, 2017. https://www.verywell.com/ how-much-does-the-hpv-vaccine-cost-514124.

Food and Drug Administration. "Current Good Manufacturing Practice for Finished Pharmaceuticals." *Code of Regulations Title 21 Volume 4.* Washington, D.C.: United States Food and Drug Administration, April 1, 2018.

Finley, Veronda M. "Patient Satisfaction in Managed Care." *http:// digitalscholarship.unlv.edu/thesesdissertations.* March 2001. http://digitalscholarship.unlv.edu/thesesdissertations/734.

Fiscal Policy Institute. "Escalating Prescription Drug Costs: The Reality and Options for Reform." Testimony Presented to the New York State AFL-CIO Task Force on Prescription Drugs, 2002.

Flannery, John and Kurukchi, Geraldine. "Caring for Patients with Chronic and Complex Care Needs: The AMA Proposes a Better Way." Australian Medical Association. *ama.com.au.* April 29, 2010. https://ama.com.au/media/caring-patients-chronic-and-complex-care-needs-ama-proposes-better-way.

Forbes, Steve. "The Horrid Economic Consequences of World War I -- We Still Suffer From Them." *Forbes Media.* August 14, 2014. https://www.forbes.com/sites/steveforbes/2014/08/02/ economic-consequences-of-the-great-war/#7eac6c6d2b21.

Ford, ES, Ajani, UA, et al. "Explaining the Decrease in U. S. Deaths from Coronary Disease, 1980-2000." *New England Journal of Medicine* (2007): 2388.

Fost, Norman. "Who should Get the Last Ventilator?" *Future-Tense*. April 3, 2020. https://slate.com/technology/2020/04/coronavirus-ventilator-ethical-guidelines.html.

Ganz, Melissa. "The Medicare Prescription Drug, Improvement, & Modernization Act Of 2003: Are We Playing The Lottery With Healthcare Reform?" *3 Duke Law & Technology Review* (2004): 1-20.

Gawande, Atul. *Being Mortal: Medicine and What Matters in the End*. New York, New York: Picador USA, 2014.

Gerish, Mary. "Health Care As a Human Right." *Human Rights Magazine* 43, no. 3 (August 1, 2018).

Gerteis, Margaret, Susan Edgman-Levitan, Jennifer Daley, and Thomas L. Delbanco, editors. *Through Patient Eyes: Understanding and Promoting Patient-Centered Care*. New York, New York: Jossey-Bass, 1993.

Gitlen, Jeff. "Average Medical School Debt." *Lendeu.com*. February 15, 2017. https://lendedu.com/blog/average-medical-school-debt/.

Glover, Lacie. "Oncologists Worry About Rising Costs of Cancer Treatment." *U.S. News and World Report*. July 1, 2015. https://health.usnews.com/health-news/patient-advice/articles/2015/07/01/oncologists-worry-about-rising-costs-of-cancer-treatment.

Goldman, Dana P., et al. *Regulating Drug Prices*. Research Brief, Santa Monica, CA: RAND Corporation, 2008.

"Good Samaritans Law and Legal Definition." *USLegal.com*. 2016. https://definitions.uslegal.com/g/good-samaritans/.

Goodman, John C. "Are High Deductibles A Good Thing? Part 1." *Forbes.com*. March 7, 2016. https://www.forbes.com/sites/johngoodman/2016/03/07/are-high-deductibles-a-good-thing-part-i/#5e263d947290.

Goodnough, Abby, and Robert Pear. "Unable to Meet the Deductible or the Doctor." *New York TImes.* October 24, 2014. https://www.nytimes.com/2014/10/18/us/unable-to-meet-the-deductible-or-the-doctor.html.

Gorman, Linda. *The History of Health Care Costs and Health Insurance.* Background Research Report, Wisconsin Policy Research Institute, Inc., 2006.

Gov.UK. *New Era of Education and Training for NHS Staff.* May 28, 2013. https://www.gov.uk/government/news/new-era-of-education-and-training-for-nhs-staff.

Gray, Bradley, Jonathan Vandergrift, Rebecca S. Lipner, and Marianne M. Green. "Comparison of Content on the American Board of Internal Medicine Maintenance of Certification Examination With Conditions Seen in Practice by General Internists." *Journal of the American Medical Association* (2017): 2317-2324.

Greenstone, Gerry. "The History of Bloodletting." *BC Medical Journal* (2010): 12-14.

Greenwald, Leslie, et al. "Specialty Versus Community Hospitals: Referrals, Quality, And Community Benefits." *Health Affairs* (2006): 106-118.

Gutherz, Cheryl and Baro, Shira. "Why Patients with Primary Care Physicians Use the Emergency Department for Non-Urgent Care." *The Einstein Quarterly Journal of Biology and Medicine* (2001): 171-176.

Hanna, Kathi E., Editor. *Biomedical Politics.* Washington, D.C.: National Academy Press, 1991.

Hardaway, Andrea. *The Top 6 Reasons Process Improvement Initiatives Fail.* July 21, 2015. https://www.linkedin.com/pulse/top-6-reasons-process-improvement-operational-fail-andrea.

Hayes, John, Jeffrey L. Jackson, Gail M. McNutt, et al. "Association between Physician Time-Unlimited vs. Time-Limited Internal Medicine Board Certification and Ambulatory Patient Care Quality." *Journal of the American Medical Association* (2014): 2358-2363.

Hayes, Tara O'Neill. "Are Electronic Medical Records Worth the Costs of Implementation?" *American Action Forum.* August 6, 2015. https://www.americanactionforum.org/research/are-electronic-medical-records-worth-the-costs-of-implementation/.

Haynes, R. Bryan, et al. "Management of Patient Compliance in the Treatment of Hypertension." *Hypertension* (1982): 415-423.

Health Insurance Institute. "Source Book of Health Insurance Data 1979-1980." Washington, D.C., 1980.

Heman, Bob. "10 Statistics on Hospital Labor Costs as a Percentage of Operating Revenue." *BeckersHospitalReview.com.* December 10, 2013. http://www.beckershospitalreview.com/finance/10-statistics-on-hospital-labor-costs-as-a-percentage-of-operating-revenue.html.

Herrick, Devon M. "Unnecessary Regulations that Increase Prescription Drug Costs." *National Center for Policy Analysis.* March 7, 2013. http://www.ncpa.org/pub/st346.

American Heart Association. "Heart Failure Patients Have More Doctor Visits, Medications Than Others On Medicare." *ScienceDaily.com.* November 2008. https://www.sciencedaily.com/releases/2008/11/081112101335.htm.

Holgash, Kayla and Martha Heberlein. *Health Affairs Blog.* April 19, 2019. https://www.healthaffairs.org/do/10.1377/hblog20190401.678690/full/.

Holmes, Sarah E. "Standardized Testing and the No Child Left Behind Act." Paper, East

Carolina University, 2009.

IHS Markit LTD. "The Complexities of Physician Supply and Demand: Projections from 2017-2032." *Association of American Medical Colleges.* April 2019. https://aamc-black.global.ssl.fastly.net/production/media/filer_public/31/13/3113ee5c-a038-4c16-89af-294a69826650/2019_update_-_the_complexities_of_physician_supply_and_demand_-_projections_from_2017-2032.pdf.

Isidore, Chris, Tal Kopan, and Julia Horowitz. "Closed Puerto Rico Factories Are the Sole Source of Some Critical Drugs." *CNN Money.* September 29, 2017. https://money.cnn.com/2017/09/29/news/companies/puerto-rico-drug-makers/index.html.

Issac, Leo. "Online Learning for Sports Management." *LeoIssac.com.* 2013. http://www.leoisaac.com/budget/bud031.htm.

Jain, Sachin. *What are the Main Purposes of Advertising?* Accessed December 31, 2018. http://www.shareyouressays.com/essays/what-are-the-main-purposes-of-advertising/89394.

James, Brent C. and Gregory P. Poulsen. "The Case for Capitation." *Harvard Business Review* (2016): 102-111.

Jingfeng, Cai. "A Historical Overview of Traditional Chinese Medicine and Ancient Chinese Medical Ethics." *Ethik in der Medizin* (1998): S84–S91.

Jones, Jeffrey M. "Americans Seeing Doctors More Often." *Gallup.com.* November 30, 2004. http://www.gallup.com/poll/14194/Americans-Seeing-Doctors-More-Often.aspx.

Jones, W. H. S. *Hippocrates: Vol 1.* London: Harvard Univsersity Press, 1923.

Kate, T., S. Gauri, Pooja Sehgal, Nikhilesh Jasuja, Rupai Bansal, and Ancheta. Rommel. "HMO vs PPO." *Diffen.com.* September 3, 2017. http://www.diffen.com/difference/HMO_vs_PPO.

Ketchel, Paul. "Patient Guide: High-Deductible Health Care Plans." *Nydailyviews.com.* March 11, 2016. http://www.

nydailynews.com/life-style/patient-guide-high-deductible-health-care-plans-article-1.2561857.

Kim, Jonathan J. *Legal Information Institute.* May 2017. https://www.law.cornell.edu/wex/contract.

Kirk, Lynne M. "Professionalism in Medicine: Definitions and Considerations for Teaching." *Proceedings Baylor University Medical Center* (2007): 13-16.

KKF's State Health Facts . *Professionally Active Physician.* March 2019. https://www.kff.org/other/state-indicator/total-active-physicians/?currentTimeframe=0&sortModel=%7B%22colId%22:%22Location%22,%22sort%22:%22asc%22%7D.

KSR Publishing. "U.S. Hospitals Wrestle with Shortages of Drug Supplies Made in Puerto Rico." *Healthcarepurchasingnews.com.* October 2017. https://www.hpnonline.com/u.s.hospitals-wrestle-shortages-drug-supplies-made-puerto-rico/.

LaCombe, Michael A. "Teaching and Learning by Example." *Annals of Internal Medicine* (2018): 521-522.

Lacson, Eduardo, Norma Ofsthun, and Michael J. Lazarus. "Effect of Variability in Anemia Management on Hemoglobin Outcomes in ESRD." *American Journal of Kidney Diseases* (2003): 111-124.

Law, Michael R., Lucy Cheng, Irfan A. Dhalla, Deborah Heard, and Steven G. Morgan. "The Effect of Cost on Adherence to Prescription Medications in Canada." *Canadian Medical Association Journal* (February 21, 2012): 297-302.

Lee, Andrew, M. I. "No Child Left Behind (NCLB): What You Need to Know." *Understood for All.* 2018. https://www.understood.org/en/school-learning/your-childs-rights/basics-about-childs-rights/no-child-left-behind-nclb-what-you-need-to-know.

Leisinger, Klaus M. "Meeting the Global Health Challenge: The Role of the Pharmaceutical Industry." *Makingitmagazine.com.* October 31, 2012. http://www.makingitmagazine.net/?p=6046.

Lewis, Cliona, Emma Wallace, Lorraine Kyne, Walter Cullen, and Susan M. Smith. "Training Doctors to Manage Patients with Multimorbidity." *Journal of Comorbidity* (2016): 85-94.

Library of Congress. *Congress.gov.* 1982. https://www.congress.gov/bill/97th-congress/house-bill/4961.

Lim, Kwanghui. "The Relationship between Research and Innovation in the Semiconductor and Pharmaceutical Industries (1981–1997)." *Research Policy* (2004): 287–321.

Lincoff, Nina. "The Future of Healthcare Could Be in Concierge Medicine." *Healthline.* June 30, 2015. https://www.healthline.com/health-news/the-future-of-healthcare-could-be-in-concierge-medicine-063015#1.

LiveClinic Healthcare Blog. "What Are the Average Physician Overhead Rates in 2017?" *LiveClinic Healthcare Blog.* February 16, 2017. http://liveclinic.com/blog/practice-management/physician-overheard-rates-2017/.

Loeb, Danielle F., Ingrid A. Binswanger, Carey Candrian, and Elizabeth A. Bayliss. "Primary Care Physician Insights Into a Typology of the Complex Patient in Primary Care." *Annals of Family Medicine* (2015): 451-455.

Madden, Susanne. "Participating in New Healthcare Exchange Plans." February 19, 2014. http://www.physicianspractice.com/healthcare-reform/participating-new-healthcare-exchange-plans.

Mahoney, Joe. "New York Faces Growing Wave of COVID-19 Deaths at Nursing Homes." *The Daily Star* (Oneonta, NY), April 22, 2020.

Malcolm, Candice. "The Pitfalls of Single-Payer Health Care: Canada's Cautionary Tale ." *National Review.* April 13, 2017. https://www.nationalreview.com/2017/04/canada-single-payer-health-care-system-failures-cautionary-tale/.

Management Sciences for Health. *Evaluating the Cost of Pharmaceuticals,* training course participant guide, Arlington, Virginia: U.S. Agency for International Development by the Rational Pharmaceutical Management Plus Program, 2007.

Mark, Joshua. "Health Care in Ancient Mesopotamia." *Ancient History Encyclopedia.* May 21, 2014. https://www.ancient.eu/article/687/health-care-in-ancient-mesopotamia/.

Marks, Joshua J. "Egyptian Medical Treatments." *AncientHistoryEncyclopedia.com.* February 20, 2017. http://www.ancient.eu/article/51/.

Maxfield, John. "A Timeline of Wells Fargo's Sales Scandal." *The Motley Fool.* September 24, 2017. https://www.fool.com/investing/2017/09/24/a-timeline-of-wells-fargos-sales-scandal.aspx.

McDonnell, Ken. "History of Health Insurance Benefits." *EmployeeBenefitsResearchInstitute.org.* March 2002. https://www.ebri.org/publications/facts/index.cfm?fa=0302fact.

McNamara, Audrey. "Cuomo Warns New York Is 'Still on the Way up the Mountain' as Virus Cases Top 30,000." *CBS News.* March 25, 2020. https://www.cbsnews.com/news/new-york-cuomo-cases-over-30000/.

McPartland, Ginny. *Researchers Strive for Decades to Solve Mysteries of Total Health.* May 6, 2012. http://kaiserpermanentehistory.org/tag/chronic-disease/.

MD Toolbox. *E-Prescribing Mandate State Laws.* 2019. https://www.mdtoolbox.com/(X(1)S(yiuqjnn2xghzoovj4w3dtxvf))/eprescribe-map.aspx.

Medical News Today Editorial Team. "What Is Ancient Greek Medicine?" *www.medicalnewstoday.com.* January 5, 2016. https://www.medicalnewstoday.com/info/medicine/ancient-greek-medicine.php.

Melissa. "Doctors Aren't Actually Bound by the Hippocratic Oath." *Gizmodo.com.* November 15, 2013. https://gizmodo.com/doctors-aren-t-actually-bound-by-the-hippocratic-oath-1465044222.

Meyerhoefer, Chad D., et al. "The Consequences of Electronic Health Record Adoption for Physician Productivity and Birth Outcomes ." *ILR Review* (2016): 860-869.

Mitchell, Deborah. "Look At The History of Health Insurance in America." *Emaxhealth.com.* September 21, 2009. https://www.emaxhealth.com/1275/72/33689/look-history-health-insurance-america.html.

Modern Medical Network. "Discounting Fees for Self-Pay Patients." *PhysiciansPractice.com.* February 1, 2008. http://www.physicianspractice.com/qa/discounting-fees-self-pay-patients.

Morrow, Bob. "Interaction of Insurance and Kidney Care" (presentation, Chronic Kidney

Disease: A Deep Dive 2018, National Kidney Foundation, Houston, TX, May 18, 2018).

MRI Assist. *MRI Assist.* 2013. http://www.mri-assist.com/.

Mulero, Ana. "Gottlieb Offers Solutions for High Generic Drug Prices, Real-Time Postmarket Surveillance." *Regulatory Affairs Professionals Society.* April 25, 2018. https://www.raps.org/news-and-articles/news-articles/2018/4/gottlieb-offers-solutions-for-high-generic-drug-pr.

Murphy, Brendan. "For First Time, Physician Practice Owners Are Not the Majority." *AMA-assn.org economics.* May 31, 2017.

https://www.ama-assn.org/practice-management/economics/first-time-physician-practice-owners-are-not-majority.

Murphy, Brooke. "21 Statistics on High-Deductible Health Plans." *Beckershospital review.com*. May 19, 2016. http://www.becker-shospitalreview.com/finance/21-statistics-on-high-deductible-health-plans.html.

Murray, Jean. "Bonus Depreciation and How It Affects Business Taxes." *The Balance Small Business*. August 11, 2019. https://www.thebalancesmb.com/what-is-bonus-depreciation-398144.

—. "What is a Section 179 Deduction?" *the Balance Small Business*. Jnuary 5, 2020. https://www.thebalancesmb.com/what-is-a-section-179-deduction-397650.

National Center for Health Statistics. *Health, United States, 2015: With Special Feature On Racial and Ethnic Health Disparities*. Hyattsville, Maryland: United States Government Printing Office, 2016.

National Council on Disability. "Appendix B. A Brief History of Managed Care ." *NCD.gov*. 2013. http://www.ncd.gov/publications/2013/20130315/20130513_AppendixB.

National Education Association. *History of Standardized Testing in the Unitied States*. 2017. http://www.nea.org/home/66139.htm.

National Institute of Health. *Kidney Disease Statistics for the United States*. December 2016. https://www.niddk.nih.gov/health-information/health-statistics/kidney-disease.

National Sanitarium Association. "A Short History of the National Sanitarium Association (NSA)." *nationalsanitarium.ca*. 2019. http://nationalsanitarium.ca/history.

Nelson, Lyle. *Lessons from Medicare's Demonstration Projects on Value-Based Payment*. Washington, D.C.: Congressional Budget Office, 2012.

New York Department of Health. "Advisory: Hospital Discharges and Admissions to Nursing Homes." Albany: State of New York, March 25, 2020.

New York State Task Force on Life and the Law, New York State Department of Health. *Ventilator Allocation Guidelines.* Task Force report, Albany: State of New York, 2015.

"'Nightmare' for Surgeons? Medicare Is Ending Global Payments for Surgeries, A." Advisory Board. November 13, 2014. https://www.advisory.com/daily-briefing/2014/11/13/a-nightmare-for-surgeons-medicare-is-ending-global-payments-for-surgeries.

Nordqvist, Christian. "A History Of Medicine." *Medical News Today.com.* August 9, 2012. http://www.medicalnewstoday.com/info/medicine/ancient-greek-medicine.php.

Nowbar, Alexabdra N., Mauro Gitto, James P. Howard, Darrel P. Francis, and Rasha Al-Lamee. "Mortality From Ischemic Heart Disease." *Circulation: Cardiovascular Quality and Outcomes* (June 2019): 1-11.

Ofri, Danielle. "Quality Medical Care." *New York Times.* 2017. https://danielleofri.com/quality-medical-care/.

OpenSecrets.org. *Top Industries.* October 29, 2019. https://www.opensecrets.org/lobby/top.php?indexType=i.

Orentlicher, David. "Controlling Health Care Spending: More Patient 'Skin in the Game?'" *Indiana Health Law Review* (2016): 348-362.

Orr, Robert. "Professional Oaths: History, Usage, Content and Changes." *Christian Medical and Dental Association.* March 1, 2009. https://www.cmda.org/resources/publication/tcd-spring-2009-professional-oaths.

Osborn, David K. "Galen: Greatest Physician of the Roman

Empire." *GreekMedicine.net.* 2015. http://www.greekmedicine. net/whos_who/Galen.html.

—. "Hippocrates Father of Medicine." *GreekMedicine.net.* 2015. http://www.greekmedicine.net/whos_who/Hippocrates. html.

Parente, Stephen. "Affordable Care Act Will Deliver a Big Surprise in 2017." *Pennlive.com.* December15, 2014. http://www.penn-live.com/opinion/2014/12/affordable_care_act_obamacare_1. html?ath=ff683cc1591b3e2bae51d60b23238e7c.

Parks, Jeffery. "How Algorithm Driven Medicine Can Affect Patient Care." *KevinMD.com.* January 30, 2012. https://www. kevinmd.com/blog/2012/01/algorithm-driven-medicine-af-fect-patient-care.html.

"Patient Protection and Affordable Care Act." *Wikipedia, The Free Encyclopedia.* September 12, 2019. https://en.wikipedia. org/wiki/Patient_Protection_and_Affordable_Care_Act.

Pellegrino, Edmund. "The Medical Profession as a Moral Com-munity." *Bulletin of the New York Academy of Medicine* (1990): 221-232.

Perry, Clifton B. "What Standard for the Standard HMO Gatekeeper?" *www.thefreelibrary.com.* July 1, 2001. https:// www.thefreelibrary.com/What+standard+for+the+stan-dard+HMO+gatekeeper%3f-a082881813.

Perry, Jennifer, Foster Mobley, and Matt Brubaker. "Most Doctors Have Little or No Management Training, and That's a Prob-lem." *Harvard Business Review.* December 15, 2017. https:// hbr.org/2017/12/most-doctors-have-little-or-no-management-training-and-thats-a-problem.

PEW Research. "PEW Research Center Religion & Pub-lic Life." *Views on End-of-Life Medical Treatments.* November 21, 2013. http://www.pewforum.org/2013/11/21/ views-on-end-of-life-medical-treatments/.

Pfuntner, Anne, Lauren M. Wier, and Claudia Steiner. *Costs for Hospital Stays in the United States, 2011*. HCUP Statistical Brief #168, Rockville, MD: Agency for Healthcare Research and Quality, 2013.

"Physician Patient Relationship Law and Legal Definition." *USLEGAL.com.* 2016. https://definitions.uslegal.com/p/physician-patient-relationship/.

Physicians Practice. *Physicians Practice.* July 1, 2005. http://www.physicianspractice.com/qa/billing-benchmarks.

Pinder, Jeanne. "Saving Money: Paying Cash for Health Care Even if You're Insured." *ClearHealthCosts.com.* September 4, 2014. http://clearhealthcosts.com/blog/2014/09/saving-money-paying-cash-even-youre-insured-draft/.

Porter, Sheri. "How Would You Describe a 'Complex' Patient? ." *American Association of Family Practice.* September 18, 2015. https://www.aafp.org/news/practice-professional-issues/20150918patientcomplexity.html.

Portuese, Enrico and Orchard, Trevor. *Mortality in Insulin-Dependent Diabetes.* Bethesda, Marylannd: NIH, 1995.

Price, Massoume. "History of Ancient Medicine in Mesopotamia & Iran." *IranChamber.com.* October 2001. http://www.iranchamber.com/history/articles/ancient_medicine_mesopotamia_iran.php.

Raban, Kirk. "Fair Market Value for Physician Compensation Arrangements." *Radiology Business Management Association.* Las Vegas, Nevada, 2011.

Rappleye, Emily. "Top 20 Healthcare Lobbyists by Spending." *Beckerhospitalreview.com.* August 17, 2015. http://www.beckershospitalreview.com/finance/top-20-healthcare-lobbyists-by-spending.html.

Reuben, David B. and Mary E. Tinetti. "Goal-Oriented Patient Care — An Alternative Health Outcomes Paradigm." *New England Journal of Medicine* (March 1, 2012): 777-779.

Robert Michel, Host. "Aetna CEO Declares Affordable Care Act in 'Death Spiral' in a Speech of Interest to Pathologists and Medical Laboratory Professionals." *Dark Daily*. April 10, 2017. http://www.darkdaily.com/aetna-ceo-declares-affordable-care-act-in-death-spiral-in-a-speech-of-interest-to-pathologists-and-medical-laboratory-professionals-407#axzz4dzkgu2iy.

Romeo, Nick. "The Grim Ethical Dilemma of Rationing Medical Care, Explained." *Vox.com*. March 31, 2020. https://www.vox.com/coronavirus-covid19/2020/3/31/21199721/coronavirus-covid-19-hospitals-triage-rationing-italy-new-york.

Rothbaum, Peggy. "The Doctor-Patient Relationship Is Everything." *KevinMD.com*. November 22, 2017. https://www.kevinmd.com/blog/2017/11/doctor-patient-relationship-everything.html.

Sandu, Alexander T., R. Adams Dudley, and Dhruv S. Kazi. "A Cost Analysis of the American

Board of Internal Medicine's Maintenance-of-Certification Program." *Annals of Internal*

Medicine (2015): 401-408.

Sarpatwari, Ameet. "Why Many Generic Drugs Are Becoming So Expensive." *Harvard Health Blog*. October 15, 2015. https://www.health.harvard.edu/blog/why-many-generic-drugs-are-becoming-so-expensive-201510228480.

Schuyler, Michael. *Why the U.S. Postal Service Is in Greater Financial Trouble than Most Foreign Postal Services - The Role of Governement Micromanagement*. Congressional Advisory No. 282, Washington, D.C.: Institute for Research on the Economics of Taxation, 2012.

Scott, Dylan. "The Untold Story of TV's First Pre-scription Drug Ad." *STAT News.* December 5, 2015. https://www.statnews.com/2015/12/11/untold-story-tvs-first-prescription-drug-ad/.

Sekha, M. Sonal and Vyas, N. "Defensive Medicine: A Bane to Healthcare." *Annals of Medical & Health Sciences Research* (April-June 2013): 295-296.

Shumann, John Henning. "A Bygone Era: When Bipartisan-ship Led To Health Care Transformation." *National Public Radio.* October 2, 2016. https://www.npr.org/sections/health-shots/2016/10/02/495775518/a-bygone-era-when-bi-partisanship-led-to-health-care-transformation.

Smith and Howard, Certified Public Accounts and Advisors. *2018 Tax Cuts & Jobs Act Overview* . March 2018. https://www.smith-howard.com/2018-tax-cuts-jobs-act-overview/.

Snell, Melissa. "Baldwin IV." *ThoughtCo.* September 4, 2006. https://www.thoughtco.com/baldwin-iv-profile-1788372.

Social Security Administration. "Life Expectancy for Social Secu-rity." *Social Security History.* n.d. https://www.ssa.gov/history/lifeexpect.html.

—. "Notes and Brief Reports." *www.sa.gov.* 1974. https://www.ssa.gov/policy/docs/ssb/v37n3/v37n3p35.pdf.

Staiger, Douglas O., David I. Auerbach, and Peter I. Buerhaus. "Trends in the Work Hours of Physicians in the United States." *Journal of American Medical Association* (2010): 747-753.

Statista.com. "Number of Doctor Visits per Cap-ita in Selected Countries as of 2015." *Statista.com.* 2017. https://www.statista.com/statistics/236589/number-of-doctor-visits-per-capita-by-country/.

Stevens, Rosemary. "Health Care in the Early 1960s." *Health Care Financing Review* (1996): 11-22.

The Physicians Foundation. "2016 Survey of America's Physicians: Practice Patterns & Perspectives." *www.physiciansfounda-tion.org*. September 2016. https://physiciansfoundation.org/wp-content/uploads/2018/01/Biennial_Physician_Survey_2016.pdf.

Tobias Dreischulte, Tobias, et al. "Safer Prescribing — A Trial of Education, Informatics, and Financial Incentives." *New England Journal of Medicine* (2016): 1053-1064.

Torrey, Trisha. "Medicare's HCPCS Codes for Payments." *Very-WellHealth*. October 23, 2017. https://www.verywell.com/what-are-medicares-hcpcs-codes-2614952.

Tour Egypt. "The Life of Ancient Egyptians." *tourEgypt.net*. 2017. http://www.touregypt.net/historicalessays/lifeinEgypt10.htm.

Tracer, Zachary and Katherine Greifeld. "Aetna CEO: Obamacare in "Death Spiral"." *Bloomberg Business*. February 15, 2017. https://www.bloomberg.com/news/articles/2017-02-15/aetna-ceo-says-obamacare-in-a-death-spiral-with-sick-customers.

Trump, Donald J. "Executive Order on Advancing American Kidney Health." *Whitehouse.gov*. July 10, 2019. https://www.whitehouse.gov/presidential-actions/executive-order-advancing-american-kidney-health/.

Tulia, Stephanie. "Executive Coaching and the American President." *Advancing Women .com*. 2005. http://advancingwomen.com/coaching/executive_coaching_and_the_american_president.php.

"Unapproved Drugs Initiative." *Wikipedia, The Free Encyclopedia*. April 1, 2016. https://en.wikipedia.org/wiki/Unapproved_Drugs_Initiative.

U. S. Department of Health and Human Services. "Duty Hours and Patient Safety." *Agency for Healthcare Research and Quality*. August 2018. https://psnet.ahrq.gov/primers/primer/19.

U.S. Department of Health and Human Services Food and Drug Administration. *Use of Electronic Health Record Data in Clinical Investigations*. Procedural Guideline, Washington, D.C.: United States Government, 2018.

U.S. Department of Health and Human Services. *Office of Disease Prevention and Health Promotion*. November 9, 2017. https:// health.gov/hcq/.

U.S. Office of Personnel Management. *Retirement Statistics*. 2017. https://www.opm.gov/retirement-services/ retirement-statistics/.

United States Congress. "Act of July 2, 1890 (Sherman Anti-Trust Act)." *Enrolled Acts and Resolutinos of Congress, 1789-1992; General Records of the United States Government, Record Group 11*. Washington, D.C.: National Archives, July 2, 1890.

—. "An Act to Supplement Existing Laws Against Unlawful Restraints." *govtrackus.s3.amazonaws.com*. 1914. https://govtrackus.s3.amazonaws.com/legislink/pdf/stat/38/STATUTE-38-Pg730.pdf.

—. "Health Insurance Portability and Accountability Act of 1996." *Congressional Record: 142*, August 21, 1996: 1935-2103.

—. "Food and Drug Administration Safety and Innovation Act." *Congressional Record: 158*, (July 9, 2012): 993-1132.

—. "21st Century Cures Act." *Congressional Record: 162*, (December 13, 2016): 1033-1344.

—. "Public Law 115–97—December 22, 2017." *Congressional Record: 163*, (December 22, 2017): 2092.

—. "H.R. 3128 (99th): Consolidated Omnibus Budget Reconciliation Act of 1985." *Govtrack.us*. April 7, 1986. https://www.govtrack.us/congress/bills/99/hr3128/text.

—. "H.R.1 - American Recovery and Reinvestment Act of 2009."

Congress. Gov. February 17, 2009. https://www.congress.gov/bill/111th-congress/house-bill/1/text.

—. "H.R.5835 - Omnibus Budget Reconciliation Act of 1990." *Congress. Gov.* November 5, 1990. https://www.congress.gov/bill/101st-congress/house-bill/5835/text.

—. "Title 42 / Chapter 7 / Subchapter XVIII / Part B / § 1395w-4." *uscode.house.gov.* March 26, 2020. https://uscode.house.gov/view.xhtml?req=granuleid:USC-prelim-title42-section1395w-4&num=0&edition=prelim#.

United States Government. "3 Things to Know before You Pick a Health Insurance Plan." *healthcare.gov.* 2017. https://www.healthcare.gov/choose-a-plan/comparing-plans/.

United States Government Accountability Office. *GAO-16-706 Generic Drugs under Medicare.* Report to Congressional Requesters, Washington, D.C.: United States Government, 2016.

United States Government. "H.R.1 - Medicare Prescription Drug, Improvement, and Modernization Act of 2003." *Congress. Gov.* December 12, 2003. https://www.congress.gov/bill/108th-congress/house-bill/1.

—. "H.R.2 - Medicare Access and CHIP Reauthorization Act of 2015." *Congress. Gov.* 2015. https://www.congress.gov/bill/114th-congress/house-bill/2.

—. "H.R.3590 - Patient Protection and Affordable Care Act." *Congress. Gov.* 2010. https://www.congress.gov/bill/111th-congress/house-bill/3590.

United States Government. "Rules and Regulations ." *Federal Register* (2019): 9460-9463.

UnitedStatesRenalDataSystem. "Costs of ESRD." *usrds.org.* 2013. https://www.usrds.org/2013/view/v2_11.aspx.

University of Ottawa. "What is Professionalism in Medicine?"

University of Ottawa Medicine. Accessed November 6, 2017. http://www.med.uottawa.ca/Students/MD/Professionalism/eng/what_is_professionalism.html.

Unknown. "Soldier and Physician." Museo Archeologico Nazionale di Napoli. *Murals from Pompeii, Italy.* Naples, Italy, 2013.

VanLang, Christopher. "How Much of New Drug Research Is Funded by the Government Compared to Charities as Well as Pharmaceutical Companies Themselves?" *Quora.com.* October 21, 2016. https://www.quora.com/How-much-of-new-drug-research-is-funded-by-the-government-compared-to-charities-as-well-as-pharmaceutical-companies-themselves.

Vivify Health. *Turning Patients into Engaged Customers.* 2017. https://www.vivifyhealth.com/patients-to-customers/.

Wallenborn, White McKenzie. "George Washington's Terminal Illness: A Modern Medical Analysis of the Last Illness and Death of George Washington." *The Washington Papers.* November 5, 1999. http://gwpapers.virginia.edu/history/articles/illness/.

Wee, H. M., and Simon Wu. "Lean Supply Chain: Learning from the Toyota Production System." *Emerald Group Publishing Group Limited.* 2009. file:///E:/Patient%20Based%20Medical%20Care/toyota_tps2015.pdf.

Weise, Karen, Amy Fink, and Sheri Harmon. "Why Washington State? How Did It Start? Questions Answered on the U.S. Coronavirus Outbreak." *New York Times.* March 4, 2020. https://www.nytimes.com/2020/03/04/us/coronavirus-in-washington-state.html.

Wellness Directory of Minnesota. "The Nature of the Pharmaceutical Industry." *mnwelldir.org.* Accessed January 2, 2019. http://www.mnwelldir.org/docs/editorial/pharm.htm.

White, Richard D. "The Micromanagement Disease: Symptoms, Diagnosis, and Cure." *Public Personnel Management* (2010): 71-76.

Williams, Oneil. "Micromanagement's Effect on Productivity." *AZcentral.com*. 2018. https://yourbusiness.azcentral.com/micro-managements-effect-productivity-14238.html.

Wolfram, Gary. *Making College More Expensive The Unintended Consequences of Federal Tuition Aid.* Washington, D.C.: Cato Institute, 2005.

Wong, Samuel Y. S. and Albert Lee. "Communication Skills and Doctor Patient Relationship." *The Hong Kong Medical Diary* (March 2006): 7-9.

World Health Organization. *Essential Medicines and Health Products Information Portal.* December 6, 2017. http://apps.who.int/medicinedocs/en/d/Js4907e/3.8.html.

Xtelligent Healthcare Media, LLC. *How the Affordable Care Act Changed the Face of Health Insurance.* June 15, 2016. https://healthpayerintelligence.com/features/how-the-affordable-care-act-changed-the-face-of-health-insurance.

Young, Aaron, Humayun J. Chaudhry, Xiaomei Pei, Katie Arnhart, Michael Dugan, and Gregory B. Snyder. "A Census of Actively Licensed Physicians in the United States, 2016 ." *Journal of Medical Regulation* (2017): 7-21.

Young, Jeffery. *AMA Endorses Senate Healthcare Reform Bill.* December 29, 2009. http://thehill.com/homenews/senate/73249-ama-endorses-senate-health-bill.

Zamosky, Lisa. "Direct-Pay Medical Practices Could Diminish Payer Headaches." *ModernMedicine Network*. April 14, 2014. http://medicaleconomics.modernmedicine.com/medical-economics/content/tags/concierge-service/direct-pay-medical-practices-could-diminish-payer-h?page=full.

www.ingramcontent.com/pod-product-compliance
Lightning Source LLC
Chambersburg PA
CBHW071206210326
41597CB00016B/1688